BLOOM
Founded by | arihant

Olympiad ACE

A Comprehensive Practice Book
for School Olympiads & Talent Search Exams

SCIENCE
Class 4

by
Rakhi Bisht

Olympiad ACE

BLOOM

Bloom Cap Edu Ventures Pvt. Ltd.

Administrative & Production Office

'Ramchhaya' 4577/15, Agarwal Road, Darya Ganj, New Delhi -110002
Tele: 011- 47630600, 43518550

PRICE: ₹125.00

PO No. : TXT-59-T066382-08-25

Published by Arihant Publications (I) Ltd.

For further information about the books log on to
www.bloomcap.org

Follow us on

Preface

"Future belongs to those Who prepares for it today"

School Olympiads are National & International level competitions conducted by different Government, Non-Government & Educational Organisations with the purpose of making the children ready to face competitive exams.

The challenging Questions asked in Olympiads motivate them to learn more & more and bring out the best result with improved academic performance. The Awards & Scholarship offered by Olympiads motivate children to aspire & strive for doing better and emerge out to be the best.

Science Olympiads

Being a Scientist or Engineer or Doctor has always been a dream of each school going child. A good command over Science is a must for any of these. Questions of Science Olympiads are structured to help students to develop scientific temperament & motivate them to understand the concepts of science. They also focuses on improving existing knowledge of a student by adding more information.

'Bloom Science Olympiad Study Book Class 4' is a perfect resource to Study & Practice for Olympiad Exams and other National & State Level Talent Search Exams & Other Competitions.

Some Special Features of Bloom Science Olympiad Study Books are;

- Chapterwise Exercises having different types of Objective Questions; Analytical, Applications, Remembering etc, at par with the Olympiad Level.
- Detailed Explanation for each question.
- Olympiad Pattern Practice Sets at the end.

This book is prepared by Expert Panel with the utmost care, still if you have any suggestions regarding its improvement then feel free to contact us at support@bloomcap.org. We will try to inculcate your suggestions in the further editions.

Contents

Chapter 01

Plants

Adaptation in Terrestrial Plants

Adaptations are special features that allow a plant or animal to live in a particular place or habitat. Plants growing on land are called **terrestrial plants**. Plants adapt themselves according to their habitats.

There are many different types of terrestrial plants such as

- **Hilly plants** These plants are tall, straight and have a conical shape. Their leaves are narrow and needle-shaped which does not allow snow to get deposited on them, e.g. Pine, deodar, cedar, etc.
- **Plain area** plants includes two types of trees :
  - (i) **Deciduous trees** shed their leaves in winter to protect themself from cold weather, e.g. Oak, maple, etc.
  - (ii) **Evergreen trees** remain green throughout the year, e.g. Neem.
- **Desert plants** have spines instead of leaves, they have a green stem and well-developed roots, e.g. *Cactus*.
- **Marshy plants** develop special root for breathing as their main underground roots do not get sufficient oxygen from the marshy soil. Portions of their roots comes out of the soil above water level and take oxygen from the air. These roots are called **breathing roots** or **aerial roots.**

Adaptation in Aquatic Plants

- **Floating plants** have very light roots, which are not fixed at the bottom, They have air-filled cavities in their leaves and stems which make them, e.g. Water hyacinth.
- **Submerged or Underwater plants** are completely submerged in water, leaves are ribbon-like and stem is flexible, so as to withstand the water current, e.g. *Hydrilla*.
- **Fixed plants** remain fixed at the bottom of pond. They have big flat leaves on the surface of water and hollow stem under it, which allow them to float, e.g. Lotus.

Let's Practice

1. Identify the type of root given in the picture below

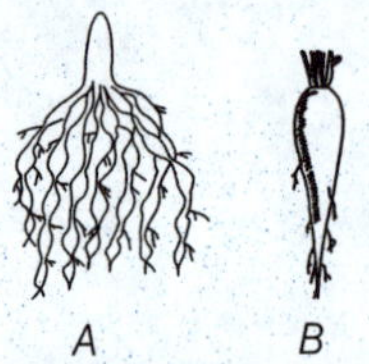

	A	B
(a)	Taproot	Fibrous root
(b)	Fibrous root	Taproot
(c)	Evergreen root	Desert root
(d)	Desert root	Evergreen root

2. Leaf prepare food for plants by the process of ....

(a) adaptation (b) absorption
(c) photosynthesis (d) chlorosynthesis

3. Look at the picture given below and identify the two gases involved.

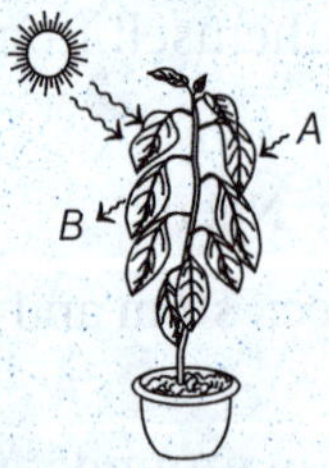

	A	B
(a)	Carbon dioxide	Oxygen
(b)	Oxygen	Carbon
(c)	Nitrogen	Oxygen
(d)	Oxygen	Nitrogen

4. In what way does the food prepared by plant is used?

(a) Some food is used by plants to grow
(b) Some food is used by plants to repair damaged parts
(c) Extra food is stored as starch and eaten by animals and humans
(d) All of the above

5. Select the incorrect option.

(a) Flower : Cauliflower (b) Fruit : Mango
(c) Stem : Sugarcane (d) Root : Potato

6. In which form does the plant store its extra food?

(a) Glucose (b) Simple sugar
(c) Starch (d) Both (a) and (c)

7. Match the type of terrestrial plants with their specific features.

	Column I		Column II
A.	Coniferous trees	1.	Remain evergreen
B.	Mangrove trees	2.	Have cones instead of flowers
C.	Evergreen trees	3.	Shed their leaves in winter
D.	Deciduous trees	4.	Have breathing roots

Codes

	A	B	C	D		A	B	C	D
(a)	2	4	1	3	(b)	1	2	3	4
(c)	4	3	2	1	(d)	3	2	4	1

8. Study the given diagram carefully and identify the labels *A* and *B* by choosing correct option.

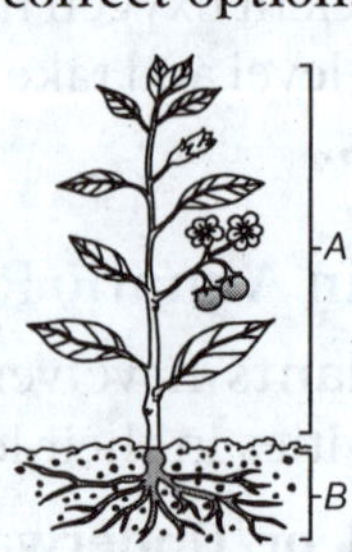

(a) *A* - Root system, *B* - Shoot system
(b) *A* - Shoot system, *B* - Root system
(c) *A* - Upper part, *B* - Lower part
(d) *A* - Stem system, *B* - Water system

9. Which of the following is the correct equation for the process of photosynthesis?

(a) $O_2 + \text{Water} \xrightarrow[\text{chlorophyll}]{\text{sunlight}} \text{Glucose} + O_2$

(b) $CO_2 + \text{Water} \xrightarrow[\text{chlorophyll}]{\text{sunlight}} \text{Starch} + CO_2$

(c) $CO_2 + \text{Water} \xrightarrow[\text{chlorophyll}]{\text{sunlight}} \text{Glucose} + O_2$

(d) $O_2 + \text{Water} \xrightarrow[\text{chlorophyll}]{\text{sunlight}} \text{Glucose} + CO_2$

10. How does *Cactus* get its food?

(a) It depends on other plants for food
(b) It is an insectivorous plant
(c) Its stem is green & waxy and prepares food for the plant
(d) It does not need food, as it can survive on atmospheric gases

11. Which of the following is not an adaptive feature of desert plant to survive?

(a) Leaves are reduced to spines to prevent loss of water
(b) Long roots are present, which go deeper in the soil in search of water
(c) They are colourless plants and do not perform photosynthesis, thus saving water
(d) None of the above

12. I am something that's thin and flat,
On a branch, I can be found,
When I'm from a deciduous
In the fall, I'm on the ground.
Guess who I am?

(a) Petals (b) Flower (c) Leaf (d) Fruit

13. Why there are no plants beyond 20 m depth underwater?

(a) They cannot respire in such great depth
(b) Plants need Sunlight to prepare food and moreover Sunlight can only reach up to depth of 20 m
(c) No man can go to such depth again and again to sow seeds of different plants
(d) All of the above

14. Why plants in hilly areas are coniferous?

(a) To prevent loss of water
(b) To prevent any damage from snow
(c) To absorb more Sunlight
(d) None of the above

15. Look at the picture given below carefully.
How does this plant *A* survive?

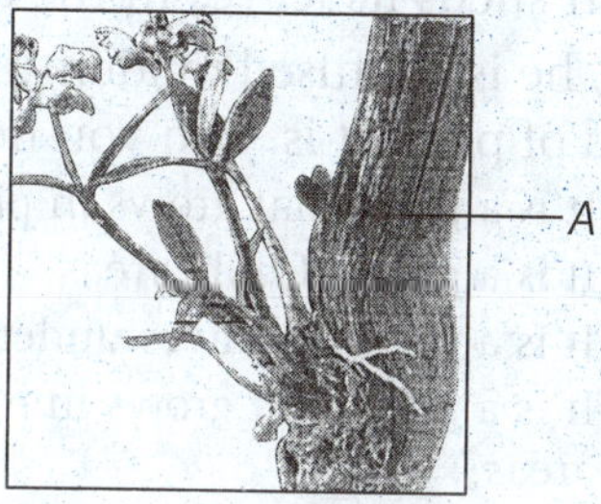

(a) They take food and water from the stem of the tree to grow
(b) They take food and water from the air by their aerial roots
(c) Gardener has to artificially supply them with food and water
(d) All of the above

16. Consider the following statements.

I. Submerged plants have ribbon-like leaves.
II. Underwater plants breathe through stomata.
III. The stem of lotus is hollow and flexible.
IV. The roots of floating plants are fixed at the bottom.

Choose the incorrect option.

(a) I and II (b) II and IV
(c) II and III (d) III and I

17. Chlorophyll is a_____coloured pigment present in the leaves of the plants.

(a) blue (b) green
(c) orange (d) red

18. Abhishek knew that plants adapt themselves to the conditions in the environment in which they live. He observed a plant and noticed the following characteristics.

(i) It has lots of branches and leaves.
(ii) It can withstand summer heat.
(iii) It sheds its leaves in the autumn.

But, he is confused to identify what kind of plant it is. Can you help him?

(a) It is a plant that grows in plains.
(b) It is a plant of hilly areas.
(c) It is a plant that lives under water.
(d) It is a plant that grows in marshy areas.

19. Which of the following have leaves without pores?

(a) Underwater plants
(b) Fixed plants
(c) Floating plants
(d) Evergreen plants

20. Study the flow chart and choose the correct option for *P* and *Q*.

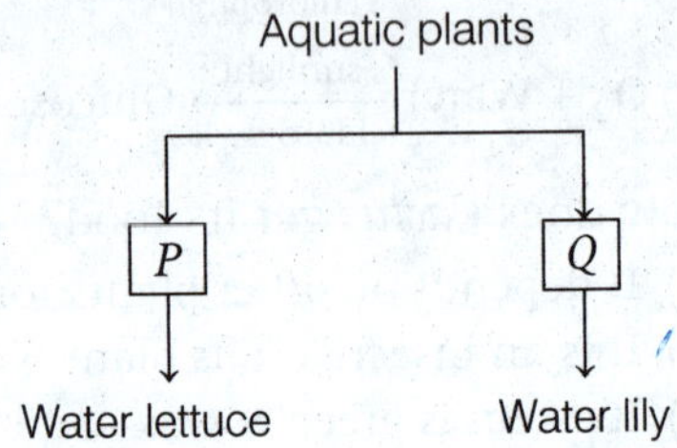

	P	*Q*
(a)	Floating	Fixed
(b)	Floating	Submerged
(c)	Submerged	Floating
(d)	Fixed	Submerged

Chapter 02

Animals

- Animals are broadly classified into two main categories
  1. **Invertebrates** They do not have a backbone, e.g. Insects, worms, snails, etc.
  2. **Vertebrates** They have a backbone and further classified into various categories.

	Vertebrates	Features	Examples
(i)	Mammals	• They have hair or fur on their body. • They give birth to young ones i.e. Viviparous. • Females produce milk.	Human, cat, horse, elephant, bats.
(ii)	Reptiles	• They have dry skin. • They have scales and not fur on their body. • They lay eggs.	Lizard, snake, turtle, alligator.
(iii)	Amphibians	• They have moist skin and webbed feet. • They live on land and in water.	Frog, toad, newt, salamander.
(iv)	Birds	• They have feathers and wings. • They lay eggs.	Sparrow, pigeon.
	• Flightless bird	• Some birds cannot fly.	Emu, ostrich, penguin.
(v)	Fish	• They breathe underwater through gills. • They have scales and fins on their body.	Rohu, guppy, shark, gold fish.

- The area where a particular animal live is called its **habitat.** To survive in habitat animals develop some specific features these changes are called **adaptation**.

Various Types of Adaptation

Terrestrial Animals

- Animals living in desert area like camels develop hump on their back to store fat and water, and have thick lips to eat prickly desert plants.
- Animals living on the tree, like monkey have long strong arms, and legs to firmly hold the branches.

Aquatic Animals

- Aquatic animals have gills instead of lungs.
- Their limbs are modified into flippers and fins to swim.
- Fishes have scales and a strong tail on their body.

Mountain and Polar Region Animals

Animals in polar region have white thick hairy coat and store fat to keep them warm, e.g. Penguin, polar bear, etc.

Birds

Birds have streamline body covered with feathers and have hollow bones.

Types of Animals (Based on Eating Habit)

- **Herbivorous** These animals eat plant only, e.g. Cow, goat, etc.
- **Carnivorous** These animals eat flesh of another animals, e.g. Lion, tiger, etc.
- **Omnivorous** These animals eat both plant and animals, e.g. Dog, cat, etc.

Mode of Reproduction in Animals

- Viviparous animals give birth to young ones, e.g. Mammals.
- Oviparous animals lay eggs, e.g. Amphibians, reptiles, fish and birds.

Life Cycle of Animals

- Life cycle of animals is the series of development of an organism in which it develop in different stages to become adult.
- Butterflies have four stages of life cycle, i.e. Egg → Larva → Pupa → Adult.
- Cockroach have three stages of life cycle, i.e. Egg → Nymph → Adult.

Food Chain

- Food chain is a linear sequence of organisms where nutrients and energy is transferred from one organisms to the other. It tell us "who eats whom?". e.g. Grass → grasshopper → frog → snake.
- The connection of multiple food chain is known as **food web.**

Let's Practice

1. Match the following animals with the term used for the group of these animals.

	Animals		Group
A.	Elephant	1.	Pride
B.	Lions	2.	Band
C.	Monkeys	3.	School
D.	Fish	4.	Herd

Codes

	A	B	C	D		A	B	C	D
(a)	4	1	2	3	(b)	3	4	1	2
(c)	2	3	4	1	(d)	1	2	3	4

2. Birds sit on their eggs to keep them warm this process is known as ....

(a) moulting (b) hatching
(c) incubation (d) warming

3. Which of the following give birth to young ones ?

(a) Lizard (b) Snake (c) Bat (d) Sparrow

4. Match the following animals as per their eating habits.

	Animals		Eating habits
A.	Dog	1.	Carnivore
B.	Leech	2.	Herbivore
C.	Elephant	3.	Omnivore
D.	Lion	4.	Parasite

Codes

	A	B	C	D		A	B	C	D
(a)	4	1	2	3	(b)	3	4	2	1
(c)	2	4	1	3	(d)	1	2	3	4

5. Amphibian in water breathe through ....

(a) gills (b) lungs
(c) skin (d) Both (a) and (c)

6. Rearrange the jumble word and answer the following question.
Process of shedding old skin by animals

L	M	N	O	T	U	I	G

(a) Reproduction (b) Moulting
(c) Incubation (d) Life cycle

7. Choose the incorrect statement.

(a) Bears have long hair on skin to keep them warm.
(b) Bears have white skin colour to reflect all the heat.
(c) Polar bears have a thick layer of fat to protect from cold.
(d) Polar bears have very good sense of smell.

8. Satya studied about structure of egg in the class. Then, he draw the diagram, but forgot to label it. Help him to label it.

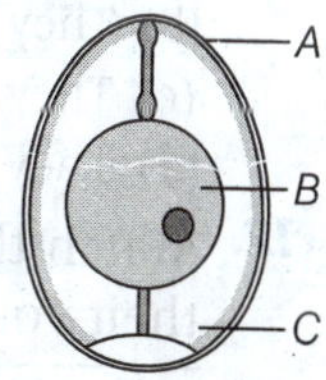

Choose the correct option.

	A	B	C
(a)	Egg membrane	Yolk	Albumin
(b)	Egg shell	Yolk	Albumin
(c)	Egg wall	Albumin	Yolk
(d)	Egg shell	Albumin	Yolk

9. Arrange the following steps of egg hatching in correct sequence.

I. Parent bird sits on the egg to keep it warm.
II. Chick breaks the shell and comes out when grown.

III. Parent bird lays eggs.
IV. Embryo develops into chick.

Choose the correct option.

(a) IV, I, II and III (b) III, IV, I and II
(c) III, I, IV and II (d) I, II, III and IV

10. Which of the following animals do not take care of their eggs to provide warmth?

Lizard, Sparrow, Hen, Turtle, Snake, Duck

Choose the correct option.

(a) Lizard, Turtle, Snake
(b) Snake, Hen, Duck
(c) Lizard, Sparrow, Duck
(d) Turtle, Snake, Sparrow

11. Which of the following characteristic does not help birds in flying?

(a) They have hollow bones which makes their body lighter
(b) They have wings and feathers
(c) They have streamlined body
(d) They have beak but no teeth

12. Match the following organisms with their young ones.

	Organisms		Young ones
A.	Cockroach	1.	Tadpole
B.	Butterfly	2.	Chick
C.	Frog	3.	Nymph
D.	Bird	4.	Cocoon

Codes

	A	B	C	D		A	B	C	D
(a)	4	1	2	3	(b)	3	4	1	2
(c)	2	4	1	3	(d)	1	2	3	4

13. **The adaptation mechanism of chameleon is**

(a) hibernation
(b) changing colours
(c) developing scaly skin
(d) migration

14. The following animals are similar as they are

Monkey, Squirrels, Garden Lizards

(a) Aerial animals
(b) Arboreal animals
(c) Aquatic animals
(d) Burrowing animals

15. The diagram below depicts life cycle of a butterfly. Identify different stages of its life correctly.

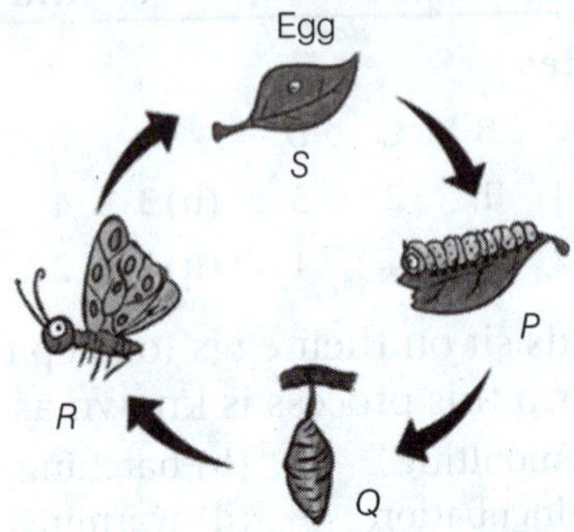

Choose the correct option.

	P	Q	R
(a)	Pupa	Larva	Adult
(b)	Adult	Larva	Pupa
(c)	Caterpillar	Larva	Adult
(d)	Larva	Pupa	Adult

16. Read the following statement carefully and identify the following A, B and C.

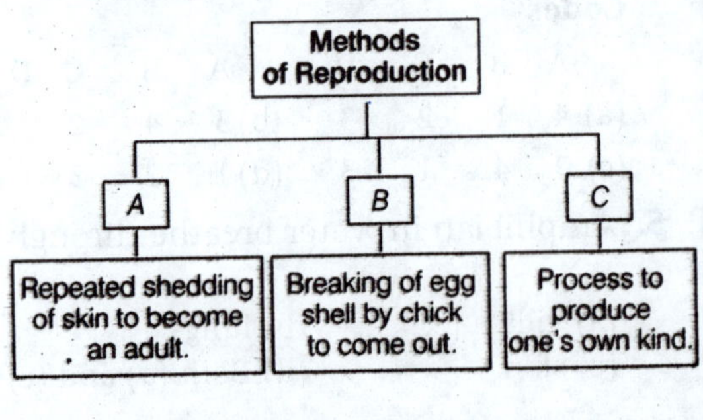

Choose the correct option.

(a) A - Reproduction, B - Moulting, C - Hatching
(b) A - Moulting, B - Reproduction, C - Hatching
(c) A - Hatching, B - Reproduction, C - Moulting
(d) A - Moulting, B - Hatching, C - Reproduction

17. Refer to given Venn diagram and choose the correct option for X.

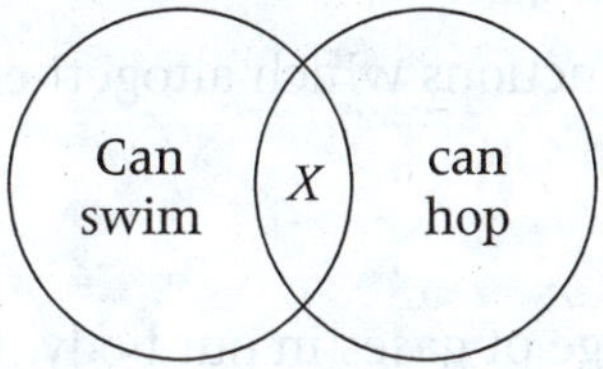

(a) Swan
(b) Duck
(c) Frog
(d) Rabbit

18. Observe the given flow chart carefully and identify which statement is correct about both X and Y.

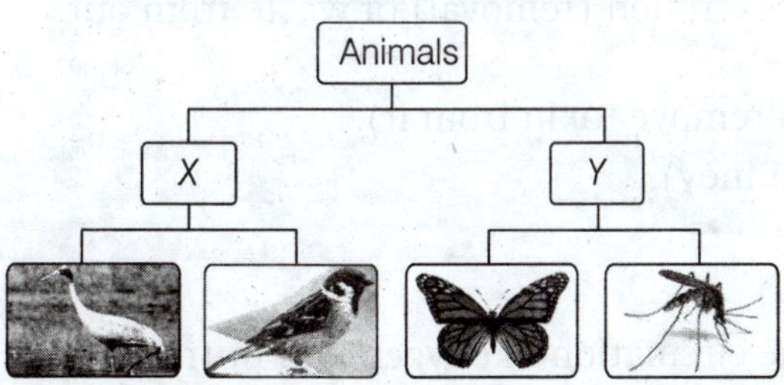

(a) Group X lay eggs, group Y give birth to young ones
(b) Group X has 3 stages life cycle, group Y has 4 stages life cycle
(c) Group X is big in size, group Y is smaller
(d) Group X give birth to young ones, group Y lay eggs.

19. I'm white but, I'm not snow.
I like to swim, but I'm not a fish.
I'm a large mammal, but I'm not a whale.
I'm furry, but I'm not a dog.
I live near the North pole, but I'm not santa.
Who am I?

(a) Penguin (b) Polar bear
(c) Arctic fox (d) Seals

20. Which of the following can be placed in the empty box to complete the given food web?

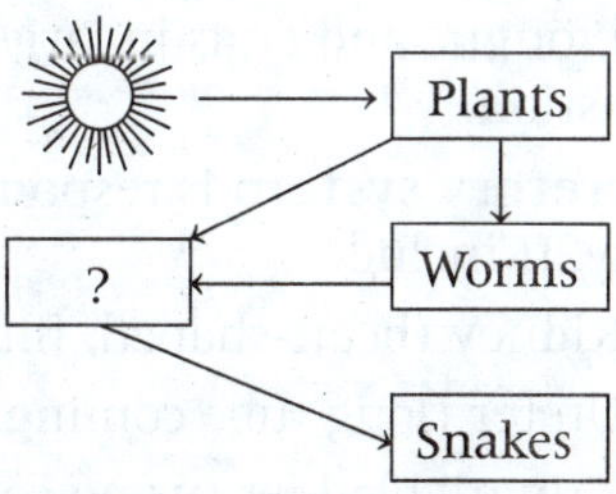

(a) Tiger (b) Hen
(c) Man (d) Vulture

Chapter 03

Human Body and Its Functioning

Human body has different organs to perform different functions which altogether form a system called **organ system**.

Various Types of Systems

1. **Respiratory system** is responsible for the exchange of gases in our body. It takes oxygen from surrounding and release carbon dioxide from our body. It includes nose, windpipe and lungs.
2. **Digestive system** is responsible for the digestion of food in our body.
   Digestion is the process of breaking down of complex food components in simpler absorbing form. The process of digestion starts from mouth, which include teeth and tongue and ends in large intestine to anus. **Liver** and **pancreas** assist in digestion.
3. **Excretory system** is responsible for the excretion (removal) of waste from our body. It includes.
   - Kidney (bean-shaped, filter blood and remove toxin from it).
   - Ureter (long tube coming from each kidney).
   - Urinary bladder (urine collects here).
   - Urethra (removes urine from the body).
4. **Circulatory system** is responsible for the circulation of oxygen and nutrients to all parts of body, through blood.
   - Heart (pumps the blood into blood vessels) and
   - Blood vessels (carry blood).
5. **Skeleton system** is responsible for the shape and support to our body. It is made up of bones and cartilages. They protect our internal organs, e.g. Skull protects our brain, ribs protects our lungs and heart.
   Teeth are considered part of the skeleton system even through they are not bone. Teeth are the strongest substance in our body being made up of **enamel** and dentine. There are 32 teeth in an adult and 28 in children. There are 4 types of teeth incisors, canine, premolars and molars.

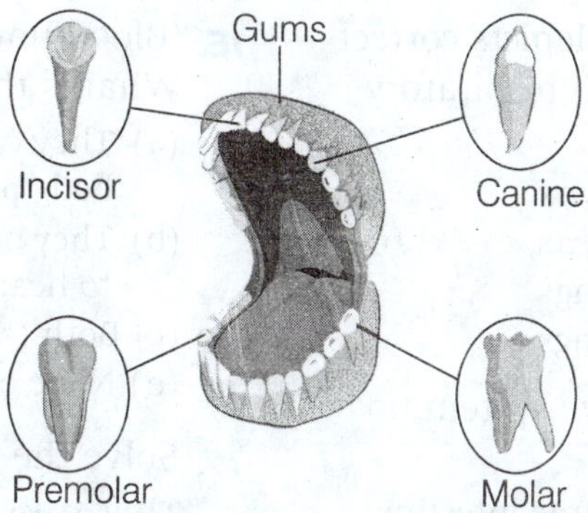

Types of teeth	No. of teeth	Functions of teeth
1. Incisors	8	Cutting and biting of food
2. Canine	4	Tearing of food
3. Premolars	8	Chewing and crushing of food
4. Molars	12	Grinding of food

6. **Nervous system** is responsible for the coordination of our body, it controls all our actions like walking, writing, swallowing, etc. It mainly consist of brain and nerves.

Let's Practice

1. Find odd one out.
(a) Stomach (b) Food pipe
(c) Windpipe (d) Small intestine

2. Which system do heart belongs to?
(a) Respiratory (b) Circulatory
(c) Digestive (d) Nervous

3. The dental formula for an adult human is
(a) $\frac{2123}{2132}$ (b) $\frac{2112}{2112}$ (c) $\frac{2123}{2123}$ (d) $\frac{2128}{2128}$

4. How many pairs of ribs are present in human skeleton system?
(a) 12 (b) 10
(c) 15 (d) 8

5. Which structure prevent the entry of food into windpipe?
(a) Larynx (b) Oesophagus
(c) Epiglottis (d) Trachea

6. In which part of digestive system protein digestion takes place?
(a) Mouth (b) Stomach
(c) Small intestine (d) Large intestine

7. Rearrange the following scrumble words with the help of clues given.
Complete digestion takes place

I	L	L	M	I	S	A	N	E	T	S	T	N	E

(a) Large intestine (b) Stomach
(c) Small intestine (d) Mouth

8. Which part of excretory system filters the blood?
(a) Kidney (b) Urethra
(c) Urinary bladder (d) Ureter

9. Which of the following prevent dust particles getting into respiratory tract?
(a) Epiglottis (b) Windpipe
(c) Small hair in nose (d) Lungs

10. Which of the following depicts correct movement of air through respiratory system?
(a) Lungs → Nose → Pharynx
(b) Nose → Lungs → Pharynx
(c) Nose → Pharynx → Lungs
(d) Pharynx → Nose → Lungs

11. In which part of digestive system no digestion occurs?
(a) Small intestine (b) Large intestine
(c) Mouth (d) Stomach

12. What is the length of small intestine in human body?
(a) 20 feet (b) 24 cm
(c) 22 feet (d) 25 feet

13. Read the following statements.
I. Blood carries hydrogen from heart to all parts of body.
II. The gastric juice help in digestion of food.
III. Small intestine absorbs water only.
Identify the true (T) and false (F) statement from the above.

Codes

	I	II	III		I	II	III
(a)	T	F	T	(b)	F	F	T
(c)	T	T	F	(d)	F	T	F

14. What is represented by *A*? Name the organ.

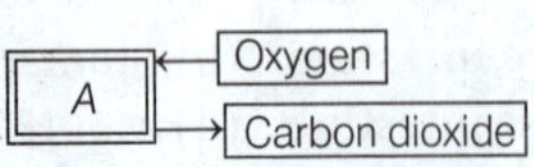

(a) Heart (b) Liver
(c) Lungs (d) Brain

15. Identify the relation
Brain : Nervous system :: ...... : Circulatory system
(a) Bone (b) Blood vessels
(c) Kidney (d) Lungs

16. 'Blood flows through blood vessels'. What is the function of blood vessels?
(a) They carry blood from heart to all body parts
(b) They carry blood from all body parts to heart
(c) Both (a) and (b)
(d) None of the above

17. Solve the riddle given below.
These are parts of your body,
sometimes they are large,
sometimes they are little,
They are white and they can be broken and in some people, they are brittle.
(a) Rib cage
(b) Blood
(c) Bone
(d) Intestine

18. Complete the given excretory system by filling up *P*, *Q*, *R* and *S*.

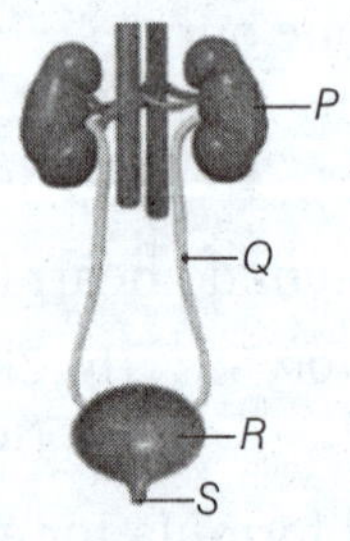

Codes

	P	*Q*	*R*	*S*
(a)	Kidneys	Ureter	Urinary bladder	Urethra
(b)	Urethra	Ureter	Urinary bladder	Kidneys
(c)	Ureter	Urethra	Kidneys	Urinary bladder
(d)	Urethra	Urinary bladder	Ureter	Kidneys

19. Refer to the given figure choose which statement is correct regarding *X* and *Y*?

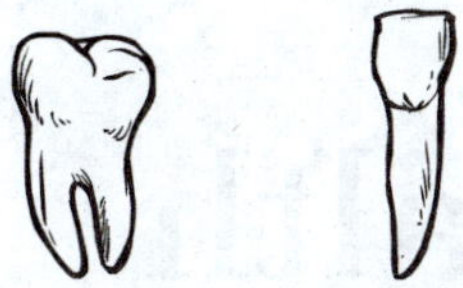

(a) *X* - Used to grind the food,
Y - Used to tear the food

(b) *X* - Used to chew the food,
Y - Used to tear the food

(c) *X* - Used to tear the food,
Y - Used to cut the food

(d) *X* - Used to chew the food,
Y - Used to bite the food

20. How many kidneys do we have?
(a) 2 (b) 3 (c) 4 (d) 1

21. Which of the following is the hardest part of our body?
(a) Ribs (b) Enamel
(c) Blood vessels (d) Intestine

22. Choose the odd one out.
(a) Molar
(b) Canines
(c) Incisors
(d) Cavity

23. Which of the following is an incorrect match?
(a) Ureters : Carry urine from kidney
(b) Incisor : Cut food
(c) Saliva : Absorbs nutrients
(d) Brain : Controls action

24. .... holds our teeth.
(a) Gum
(b) Tongue
(c) Skin
(d) Lips

25. Which part of our body regulates our walking, eating and talking etc.
(a) Our skin
(b) Our heart
(c) Our brain
(d) Our lungs

Chapter 04

Food and Health

- The components present in our food which provide us energy, help us to grow, maintain our body health are called **nutrients**.

Nutrients	Functions and Sources
1. **Carbohydrates** (energy giving food)	• Provide energy to body. Wheat, potato, rice, sugar are source of carbohydrate. Starch and sugar are the two form of it.
2. **Fats** (energy giving food)	• Provide more energy than carbohydrates, but excess of fat causes obesity. Oil, ghee, butter, etc. are rich in fats.
3. **Proteins** (body building food)	• Help in building our body, repair damage, help in growth of our body. Pulses, egg, cheese, milk, etc. are rich in protein.
4. **Vitamins** and **Minerals** (protective food)	• Vitamins keep us healthy and help us to fight against diseases. Fruits and vegetables are rich in vitamins. Vitamin-A - (keeps our eyes healthy.), Vitamin-B - (good for muscles). Vitamin-C - (makes our gums healthy) and Vitamin-D - (makes our teeth and bones healthy). • Minerals are necessary for the development of our bones and teeth. They also help in the formation of new blood in our body, e.g. Iron, calcium, iodine, etc.
5. **Roughage**	• These are the **dietary fibres** obtained from fruits, wheat, oatmeals, etc. • They help our body to get rid of undigested food.
6. **Water**	• It helps in absorption of nutrients and help in throwing out waste from our body as urine and sweat.

- **A balance diet** contain all types of nutrients including roughage and water.
- Deficiency of any nutrient can cause disease called **deficiency disease**.

Deficiency Disease

Vitamin/Minerals	Deficiency Disease	Symptoms
Vitamin-A	Loss of vision	Poor vision
Vitamin-B	Beri-Beri	Weak muscles
Vitamin-C	Scurvy	Bleeding gums
Vitamin-D	Rickets	Soft and bent bones
Calcium	Bone and tooth decay	Weak bones, tooth decay
Iodine	Goitre	Swollen glands in the neck
Iron	Anaemia	Weakness

Let's Practice

1. What are energy giving food?
(a) Carbohydrates and protein
(b) Protein and fats
(c) Fats and carbohydrates
(d) Only fats

2. Weight : 255 kg

What would you call the condition of this person?
(a) Obesity (b) Headache
(c) Malaria (d) Anaemia

3. To which categories do calcium, iron and iodine belongs to
(a) protective food (b) minerals
(c) vitamins (d) protein

4. Find the odd one.
(a) Butter (b) Oil
(c) Vegetable (d) Ghee

5. Food have various .... that keeps us healthy.
(a) components (b) substance
(c) nutrients (d) All of these

6. The body store energy in the form of ....
(a) proteins (b) fats
(c) carbohydrates (d) vitamin

7. Identify the given food item and choose the correct option for X and Y.

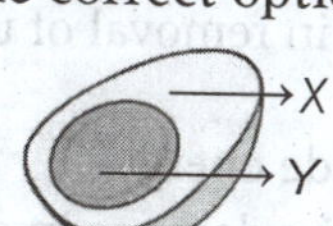

	X	Y
(a)	Protein	Carbohydrates
(b)	Fats	Protein
(c)	Protein	Fats
(d)	Vitamin	Minerals

8. Which of the following vitamin is prepared in our body with the help of Sunlight?
(a) Vitamin-A (b) Vitamin-B
(c) Vitamin-D (d) Vitamin-K

9. Which of the following statement is correct about contamination?
(a) Contamination is caused by the entry of germs by an insect bite.
(b) Contamination is caused by the entry of germs by an animal bite.
(c) Contamination is caused by the entry of germs into drinking water or edible foods.
(d) None of the above

10. Which of the following is incorrect about water?
(a) About 95% of our body is made up of water
(b) We lose lots of water through urine and sweat
(c) Water helps to maintain our body temperature
(d) We should drink atleast 6-8 glasses of water per day

11. How can following food items be preserved?

A.	Milk	1.	Dehydration
B.	Meat	2.	Salting
C.	Pickles	3.	Freezing
D.	Peas	4.	Boiling

Codes

	A	B	C	D		A	B	C	D
(a)	1	3	2	4	(b)	2	3	4	1
(c)	3	4	2	1	(d)	4	3	2	1

12. What are protective food?
I. Green leafy vegetables
II. Potatoes
III. Milk and milk product
IV. Pulses
Choose the correct option.
(a) I and III (b) I and II
(c) II and IV (d) Only III

13.

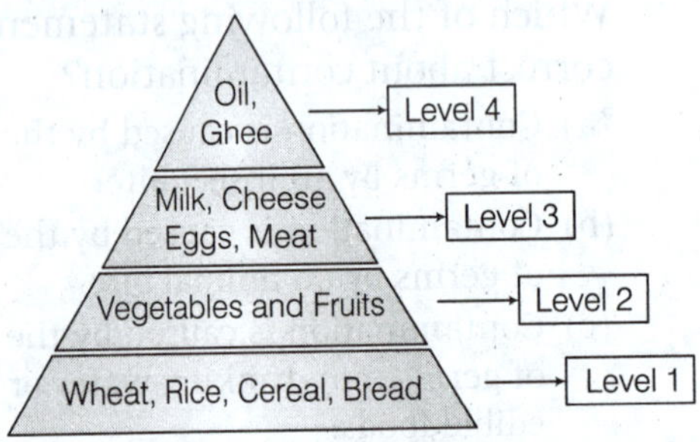

The above diagram represents different levels showing the main constituents in a balanced diet for each level.
Choose the correct option.

	Level 1	Level 2	Level 3	Level 4
(a)	Carbo-hydrates	Vitamins and minerals	Proteins	Fats
(b)	Fats	Carbo-hydrates	Proteins	Vitamins and minerals
(c)	Vitamins and minerals	Fats	Carbo-hydrates	Proteins
(d)	Proteins	Vitamins and minerals	Fats	Carbo-hydrates

14. Match the following vitamins with their uses.

Column I	Column II
A. Vitamin-A	1. Makes teeth and bones strong
B. Vitamin-B	2. Makes gums strong and heals wounds faster
C. Vitamin-C	3. Good for muscles and nerves
D. Vitamin-D	4. Keeps eyes and skin healthy

Codes

	A	B	C	D		A	B	C	D
(a)	1	3	2	4	(b)	4	3	2	1
(c)	3	4	2	1	(d)	4	2	3	1

15. We should not eat food from stalls because it contains
I. Germs
II. Mosquitoes
III. Dust
IV. Flies
Codes
(a) I and II
(b) I, III and IV
(c) Only II
(d) II and III

16. For proper digestion of food,
I. we should have food at random hours of time.
II. we should eat balanced food.
III. we should eat slowly and chew food well.
Choose the correct option.

	I	II	III		I	II	III
(a)	T	T	T	(b)	T	T	F
(c)	F	F	T	(d)	F	T	T

17. Which of the following is a function of roughage?
(a) Protects body from disease
(b) Help in removal of undigested food
(c) Provide energy
(d) Repairs damage in our body

18. Students of class IVth make some statements. Identify the student, who made the incorrect statement.

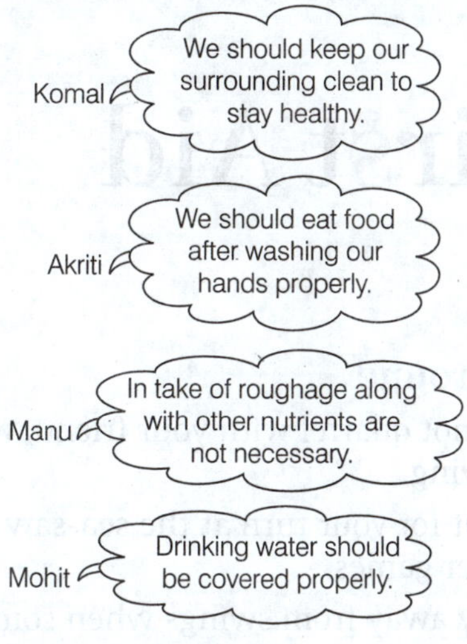

(a) Komal (b) Akriti (c) Manu (d) Mohit

19. Read the following flow chart carefully and identify which groups is/are wrong.

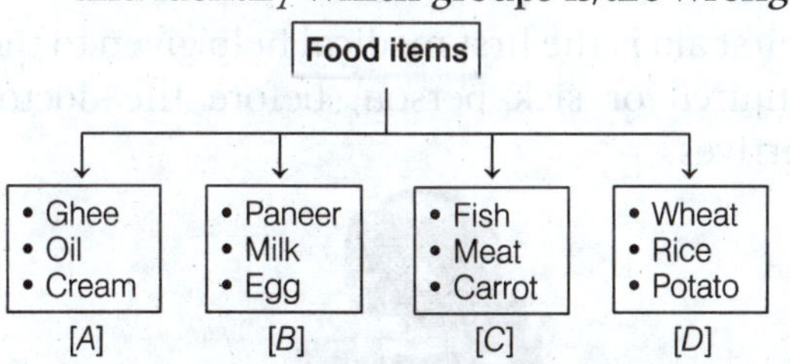

(a) *A* and *B* (b) *C* and *D*
(c) Only *B* (d) Only *C*

20. Refer to the Venn diagram given below

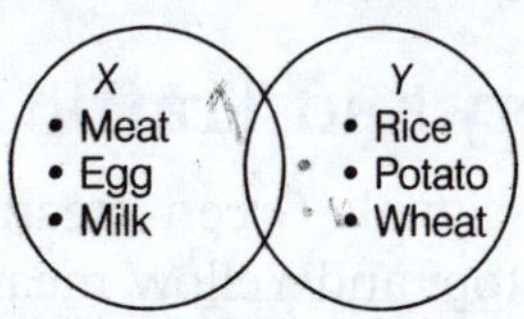

Choose the correct option for *X* and *Y*.

(a) *X* - Protein, helps in muscle and bone development, *Y*-Carbohydrates, provide energy to our body

(b) *X* - Protein, provides more energy than fats, *Y* - Fats, provide protection

(c) *X* - Vitamins, build immunity, *Y* - Minerals, build bones and teeth strong.

(d) *X* - Fats, provide immunity, *Y* - Proteins, build muscles and bone strong.

21. Boiling the milk
(a) improves taste
(b) gives more energy
(c) kills germs
(d) is not good for health

22. A runner participating in a race takes some glucose just before the race begins. This means that glucose
(a) makes running easier
(b) builds muscles instantly
(c) gives energy instantly
(d) stop sweating of the body

23. Arrange the following nutrients in ascending order of amount of energy in them.

(i) Roughage (ii) Protein
(iii) Fats (iv) Carbohydrates

(a) (i) → (iv) → (ii) → (iii)
(b) (i) → (ii) → (iv) → (iii)
(c) (iii) → (iv) → (ii) → (i)
(d) (iii) → (iv) → (i) → (ii)

24. Refer to the given Venn diagram and choose the correct option for *X* and *Y*.

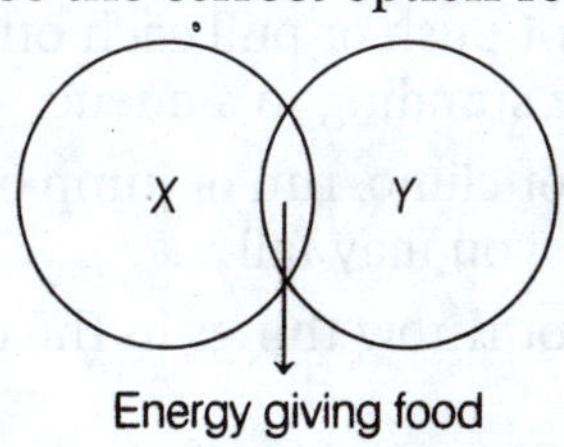

	X	*Y*
(a)	**Fats**	**Minerals**
(b)	**Carbohydrates**	**Protein**
(c)	**Carbohydrates**	**Fats**
(d)	**Minerals**	**Proteins**

Chapter 05

Safety and First Aid

Safety Rules

One should always follow safety rules at home, at school, on road and on playground.

At Home

(i) Do not play with sharp objects like knife, scissors, etc.

(ii) Never touch electric appliances with wet hands.

(iii) Do not light fire crackers alone always take help with your elders.

(iv) Never take any medicine unless your parents or a doctor gives it to you.

At School

(i) Do not run, while going up and down in the stairs.

(ii) Do not push or pull each other while standing in a queue.

(iii) Do not climb, run or jump on your desk, you may fall.

(iv) Do not throw things in the class.

On Road

(i) Always use zebra crossing while crossing road.

(ii) Do not run or play on road.

(iii) Always obey the traffic light.

(iv) Always walk on the footpath.

In Playground

(i) Do not quarrel with your friend, while playing.

(ii) Wait for your turn at the sea-saw or in other games.

(iii) Stay away from swings when someone is using them.

First aid

- First aid is the first medical help given to the injured or sick person, before the doctor arrives.

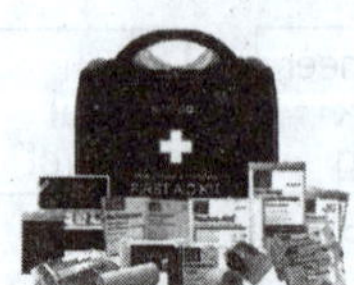

- First aid box contains-scissors, band-aid, antiseptic lotion, cotton roll, etc.

Road Safety and Traffic Rules

- Know your signals Green means 'go', Red means to 'stop' and Yellow means to 'slow down' your vehicles.
- Stop, look and then cross the road.
- Use helmets, seat belt and safety gears.
- Do not put any part of the body outside the window of a moving vehicles.
- Follow the speed limit and traffic signs.

Let's Practice

1. Choose the option for the missing term.
Fire engine : Fire : : Ambulance : ?
(a) Patients (b) Floods
(c) Storms (d) None of these

2. In case of minor burn what should be done?
(a) Pour hot water on it
(b) Pour cold water on it
(c) Pour warm water on it
(d) Apply ointment only

3. Look at the table below and find out how many things can you find in a first aid kit?

Cotton	Utensil	Adhesive bandage	Scissors	Aspirin
Knife	Antiseptic	Magazines	Tweezers	

(a) 6 (b) 3 (c) 5 (d) 4

4. Which of the following should be in a first aid kit for a child?
(a) A thermometer, ORS powder
(b) Antiseptic cream and bandages in case he cuts himself
(c) Sterile cotton
(d) All of the above

5. Which safety measures should you follow on the playground?
I. Follow the rules of whichever game you play.
II. Do not hit others with a bat or ball or anything.
III. Stand in front of the swing for your turn.
Choose the correct option.
(a) Only I (b) Only II
(c) I and II (d) II and III

6. Which of the following incidents can prove to be fatal?
(a) Touching hot utensils
(b) Running in the houses
(c) Touching electric switches with wet hands
(d) Throwing objects at anyone

7. While walking on the road, if there is no footpath then, on which side of the road should we walk ?
(a) In the middle of road
(b) On the right side of the road
(c) On the left side of the road
(d) Both (a) and (c)

8. Why it is advised not to wear nylon cloth, while working in kitchen or lighting fire cracker?
(a) They are new, they may get dirty
(b) They may catch fire
(c) Both (a) and (b)
(d) None of the above

9. Which of the following is a safety measure for children to avoid accidents at home?
(a) Leave your toys and books on the floor
(b) Never open the door to a stranger
(c) Playing with knives, scissors or sharp-edged things
(d) All of the above

10. Which of the following figures indicates safe pedestrian crossing?

(a) 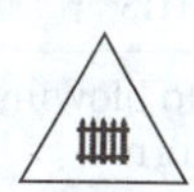

(b) 

(c) 

(d) 

11. Which of the following given safety rule is incorrect?

(a) We should not play or run in the middle of a road
(b) We should cross the road through a subway or footbridge, if available
(c) Ignore traffic signals over midnights
(d) Cross the road at the zebra crossing

12. When Gurpreet was trying to peel vegetables, he cuts his finger. What should he do as first aid at home?

(a) Rub the ice
(b) Wash the area with hot water
(c) Clean the cut with an antiseptic solution and then apply an antiseptic cream
(d) None of the above

13. While crossing the road which safety rule you would follow

(a) Don't look right and left always go straight
(b) Don't look right and left and run to cross the road
(c) Look to your right, then to your left and then again look at your right and then cross the road by using zebra crossing
(d) All of the above

14. If a person gets burnt from electricity, what first aid should be given to him?

(a) Wash the affected area with water
(b) Put an antiseptic lotion on the affected area
(c) Immediately take him to the doctor
(d) Put a band-aid on the affected area

15. Match the following items.

A.		(i)	No blowing of horn
B.		(ii)	Two way
C.		(iii)	Traffic lights
D.		(iv)	Slippery road
E.		(v)	Do not overtake

Codes

	A	B	C	D	E
(a)	(iii)	(v)	(ii)	(i)	(iv)
(b)	(v)	(iii)	(i)	(ii)	(iv)
(c)	(iii)	(ii)	(v)	(i)	(iv)
(d)	(iii)	(ii)	(v)	(iv)	(i)

16. Riya was playing in the garden. Suddenly, a honeybee bite her on her arm. Which one of the following first aid her mother should do?

(a) Remove the sting by pressing the area as early as possible
(b) Do not remove the sting, apply medicine on it
(c) Wash the area with water
(d) Put the antiseptic solution on the affected area

17. Read the following statements and choose the correct option.

Statement A Do not play with matchsticks or try to light firecrackers on your own.

Statement B Never take medicines on your own.

(a) Statement A is correct and B is incorrect
(b) Statement B is correct and A is incorrect
(c) Both the statements are correct
(d) Both the statements are incorrect

18. If there is a leakage in the gas cylinder in kitchen what precautions should your mother take?

I. Open all the windows and door.

II. Do not touch any electric switch.

III. Turn off the cylinder immediately.

Choose the correct statement.

(a) I and III
(b) II and III
(c) I and II
(d) I, II and III

19. Four students made a statement each about the safety rules they should follow in future to stay safe.

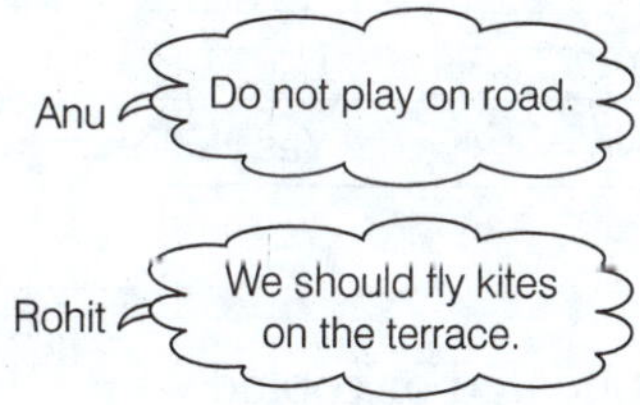

Which student did not make a correct statement?

(a) Anu
(b) Rohit
(c) Golu
(d) Sonal

20. Study the given flow chart and select the correct option regarding it.

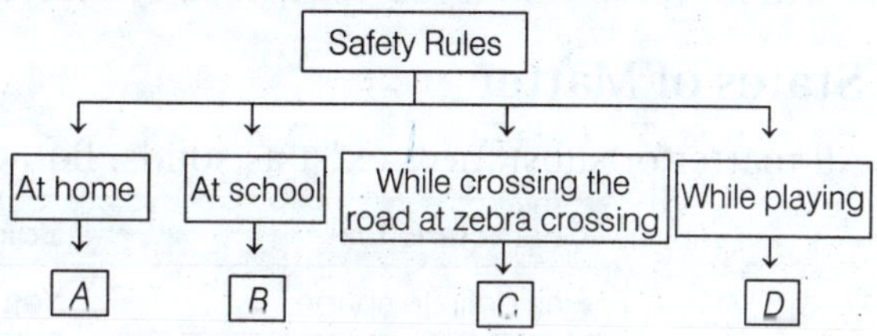

(a) *B*-Do not stand in the queue
(b) *A*-Do not touch stoves, heaters etc. when they are switched off.
(c) *D*-Do not fly kites in open fields
(d) *C*-Do not cross the road when the traffic light is green for vehicles.

Chapter 06

Matter and Materials

- Matter is anything that has mass and occupies space.
- Matter consists of tiny particles known as atoms or molecules.
- All material things are composed of matter.

States of Matter

All matter or substances exist as solids, liquids and gases.

Characteristics	Solid	Liquid	Gas
Has definite shape	Yes	No	No
Has definite volume	Yes	Yes	No
Can be compressed	No	No	Yes

Change of State of Matter

Matter can be changed from one state to another state, if heated or cooled.

- **Melting** solid converts into liquid by heating.
- **Boiling** liquid converts into gas by heating.
- **Condensation** gas converts into liquid by cooling.
- **Freezing** liquid converts into solid by cooling.
- **Evaporation** liquid converts into its vapour form.
- **Sublimation** solid converts directly into vapour form (gas) without getting change into liquid.
- **Deposition** gas converts into solid directly.

Material

Different types of matter that are used to make things are called materials. They are classified as natural or man made material.

- Material can be lustrous, hard, soft, transpatent, opaque, magnetic, non-magnetic, etc.
- Natural materials are found in nature, e.g. Air, water.
- Man made materials are artificial materials made by humans, e.g. Plastic, metals.

Let's Practice

1. Which of the following are not matter?

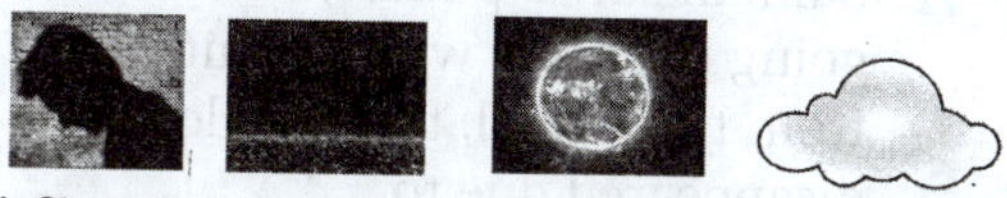

A. Shadow B. Rain C. Heat from Sun D. Cloud

Choose the correct option.

(a) *A* and *B*
(b) *B* and *D*
(c) *A* and *C*
(d) *C* and *D*

2. Which form of water is solid?

(a) Water
(b) Ice
(c) Water vapours
(d) Water flowing in rivers

3. Identify the '*X*' in the given figure.

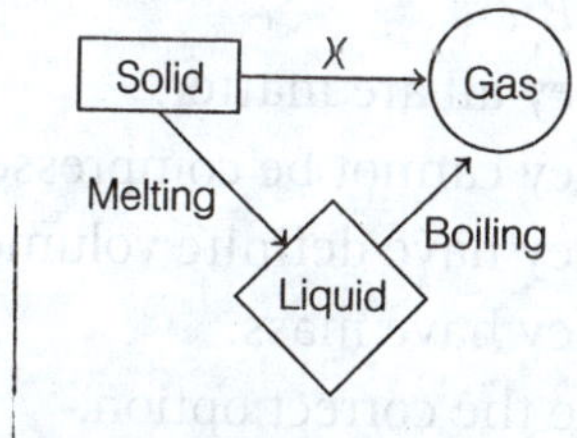

(a) Condensation
(b) Sublimation
(c) Freezing
(d) Deposition

4. Table given below shows the properties of three states of matter *A*, *B* and *C*.

Matter	Definite shape	Definite volume
A	No	Yes
B	No	No
C	Yes	Yes

Which of the following options gives the correct states of *A*, *B* and *C*?

	A	*B*	*C*
(a)	Gas	Solid	Liquid
(b)	Liquid	Gas	Solid
(c)	Gas	Liquid	Solid
(d)	Liquid	Solid	Gas

5. A liquid changes into a gas on .... and the process is called ....

(a) heating , sublimation
(b) cooling, boiling
(c) heating, boiling
(d) cooling, condensation

6. The given picture shows the process of

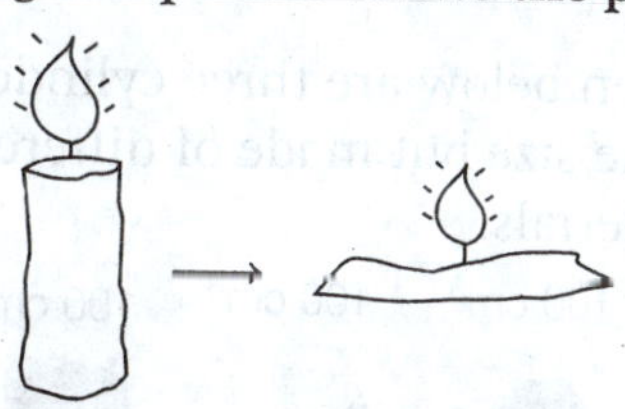

(a) Freezing (b) Melting
(c) Evaporation (d) Condensation

7. Match the given columns as per the process involved in the conversion of states:

	Column I		Column II
A.	Milk → ice cream	1.	Evaporation
B.	Clouds → raindrops	2.	Condensation
C.	Water vapours → clouds	3.	Precipitation
D.	Ice → water	4.	Melting
		5.	Freezing

Codes

	A	B	C	D		A	B	C	D
(a)	1	2	3	4	(b)	4	1	2	3
(c)	2	1	4	5	(d)	5	3	2	4

8. Observe the classification of matter as shown below carefully.

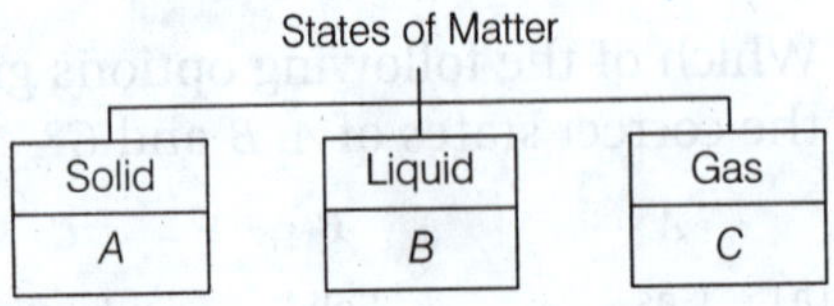

In which of the boxes snowflakes belong?

(a) Only *A* (b) Only *B*
(c) *A* and *C* (d) *B* and *C*

9. Identify the relationship of the given pair of processes and choose the missing term.

Evaporation : Condensation : : Sublimation : ?

(a) Melting (b) Freezing
(c) Deposition (d) Boiling

10. Given below are three cylinders of same size but made of different materials.

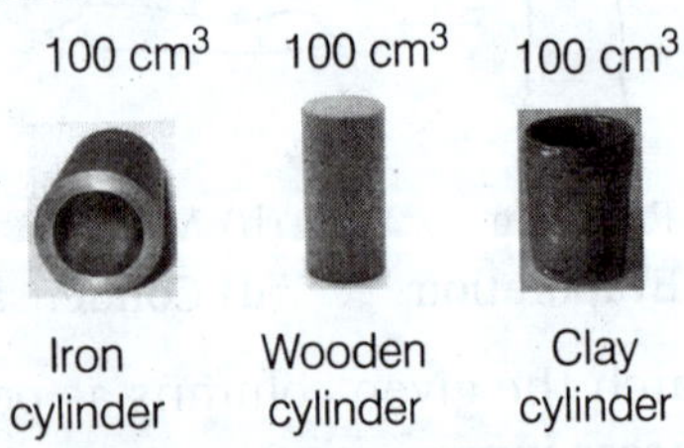

Which of the following statements about the three cylinders is correct?

(a) They all constitutes equal mass
(b) They all have same volume
(c) Only clay and iron cylinder have same mass
(d) Iron cannot be compressed but wooden and clay cylinders can be compressed

11. Identify the given relationship between states of matter and select the correct option.

Stone: Lemon Juice

(a) Table : Water vapour
(b) Salt : Sugar
(c) Watch : Milk
(d) Wood : Oxygen

12. Salman saw a puddle, when he was going to school while coming back from the school, the puddle disappeared due to

(a) melting (b) freezing
(c) condensation (d) evaporation

13. Read the given flow chart and answer the question.

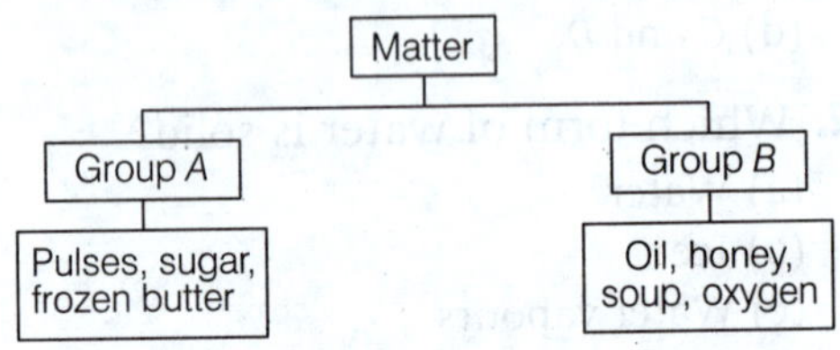

What is the similarity between objects in group *A* and objects in group *B* ?

I. They all are matter.
II. They cannot be compressed.
III. They have definite volume.
IV. They have mass.

Choose the correct option.

(a) I and II (b) I, III and IV
(c) I and IV (d) All of these

14. Two identical air filled balloons *A* and *B* were placed on each end of a rod of a weighing balance which is as shown below. Accidently, balloon *B* got punchured and air escaped out. The whole set-up is shown below

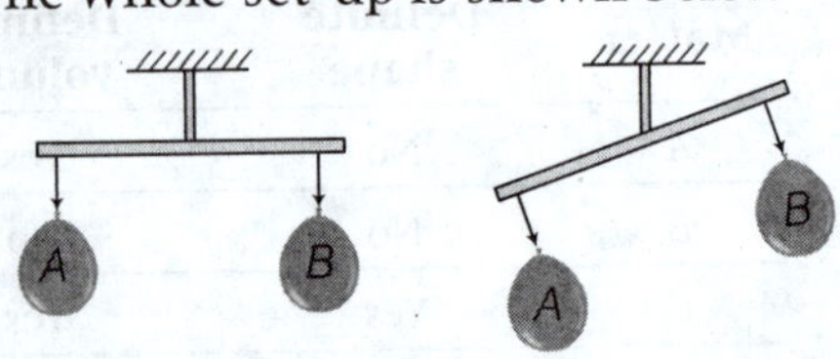

The above experiment confirms that
(a) gases have definite volume
(b) gases have no definite volume
(c) gases cannot be compressed
(d) gases have mass

15.

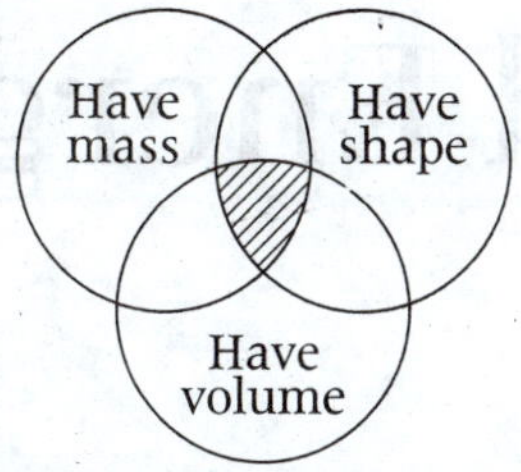

Refer to the Venn diagram given and choose the correct option for shaded region.

(a) Solids (b) Liquids
(c) Gases (d) Matter

Direction (Q.Nos 16-17) Read the given flow chart carefully and answer the questions.

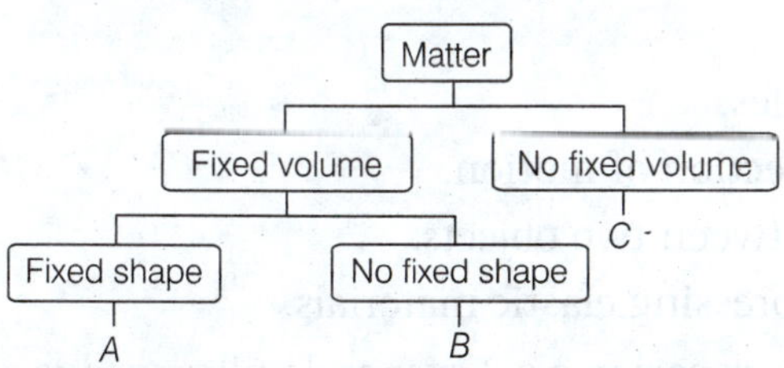

16. Which of the substance(s) is/are compressible in nature?

(a) *A* (b) *B*
(c) *C* (d) Both (a) and (b)

17. Oil and milk belongs to which type of substances, respectively?

(a) *B* (b) *B, C*
(c) *A, C* (d) Neither *A* or *C*

18. Matter changes from one state to another with. change in

(a) weight (b) height
(c) temperature (d) volume

19. Asma made a cup of tea for herself. But her phone range and she started talking on the phone. In the mean while she covered her mug of tea with a lid. After ten minutes, she removed the lid to drink tea. She observed small water droplets on the inner side of the lid. The process taking place here is

(a) melting
(b) precipitation
(c) evaporation
(d) condensation

20. Which of the following conversion is correct?

(a) Water $\xrightarrow{\text{Heat}}$ Steam $\xrightarrow{\text{Heat}}$ Ice
(b) Water $\xrightarrow{\text{Cool}}$ Ice $\xrightarrow{\text{Cool}}$ Steam
(c) Steam $\xrightarrow{\text{Cool}}$ Water $\xrightarrow{\text{Cool}}$ Ice
(d) Steam $\xrightarrow{\text{Heat}}$ Ice $\xrightarrow{\text{Heat}}$ Water

Chapter 07

Work, Force and Energy

Work

It is said to be done only when an object moves over a distance on applying force. e.g. If you move a pen, work is done but after applying lots of force, if you are not able to move a pen, no work is done.

Force

- A push or a pull acting upon an object is called a force.

  e.g. No one cannot push a ball without using force.

Various Types of Force

(i) **Muscular** Force due to the action of muscles.

(ii) **Frictional** Force acting opposite to the direction of motion.

(iii) **Gravitational** Attractive force exerting between two objects.

(iv) **Elastic** Force produced by stretching/compressing elastic materials.

- A machine is a device that uses force to make work easier. e.g, Lever and pulley wedge etc. e.g, See-saw, scissors, cars, wheels etc.

Energy

- It is defined as the capacity to do work.
- It can neither be created nor destroyed. It can only be converted from one form to another.
- There are different forms of energy. e.g. Geothermal energy, solar energy, heat energy, wind energy, sound energy etc.

Friction

- Friction is a force exerted when two surfaces are in contact with each other. We need friction to do almost all our daily task like walking, writing, running, holding things, etc.
- Every moving thing stops due to friction as the direction of force of friction is always opposite to the direction of movement of object. A rough surface has more friction than smooth surface.

Let's Practice

1. This simple machine uses a grooved wheel and a rope to carry a load.
(a) Lever
(b) Inclined plane
(c) Wheel and axle
(d) Pulley

2. Which of the following is an example of simple machine being used to do work?
(a) A girl eating a sandwich
(b) A lady going to second floor of a building using stairs
(c) A boy runs across a ground
(d) A shopkeeper counting money

3. Which of the following action/activities are done with the support of gravitational force?

1.

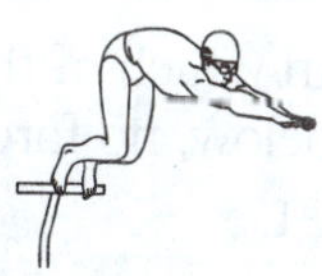
2.

3.

4.

(a) 1, 4 (b) 3, 4 (c) 2, 4 (d) 1, 3

4. This simple machine uses a slanted surface connected from a lower level to a higher level used to carry load through a height.
(a) Screw (b) Wedge
(c) Lever (d) Inclined plane

5. A fork shown in figure below is an example of which type of simple machine?

(a) Wedge (b) Lever
(c) Screw (d) Pulley

6. Which of the following process is not considered as a force?
(a) Friction (b) Weight
(c) Gravity (d) Height

7. Which of the following is/are example(s) of a pulley system?
I. Crane lifting a box
II. Elevator
III. Well lifting bucket

Codes
(a) Only I (b) Only II
(c) Only II (d) All of these

8. In which of the following examples given below, wheel and axle are not used?
I. Car steering wheel II. Door knob
III. Scissor

Codes
(a) Both I and II (b) Both II and III
(c) Only III (d) Both I and III

9. In order to keep a jar at the top most slab of kitchen, Geeta used a wooden staircase as shown in figure below.
Which type of simple machine she used?

(a) Wedge (b) Staircase

(c) Inclined plane (d) Either (a) or (b)

10. Which of the following statements are true (T) and which ones are false (F)?

1. Friction develops when two things are kept apart.
2. In order to move an object, the push or pull should be greater than friction.
3. We can walk without friction.
4. Friction slows down movements.

Codes

	1	2	3	4		1	2	3	4
(a)	F	T	F	T	(b)	F	F	T	F
(c)	T	F	F	T	(d)	F	F	T	T

11. Which of the following machines shown below is/are example(s) of wheel and axle?

I.  II. 

III. 

(a) Only I (b) Only II

(c) II and III (d) All of these

12. Given below is a diagram of lever.

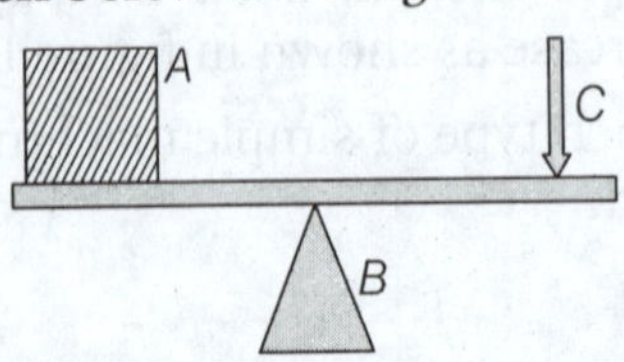

Which object is similar to the machine as shown above?

(a)  (b) 

(c) 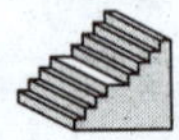 (d) 

13. In order to pull apart a nail from the wall, which of the following simple machine should be used?

(a) 

A lever such as claw ended hammer

(b) 

A wedge such as claw ended hammer

(c) 

A lever such as screw driver

(d) None of the above

14. In which of the following cases shown below, no force is being applied?

I. 

Boy pushing the wall

II. 

Boy carrying a heavy box

III. 

Book lying on table

Codes

(a) Only I (b) Only II
(c) Only III (d) All of these

15. Which principle of simple machine is used in a bottle cap shown below?

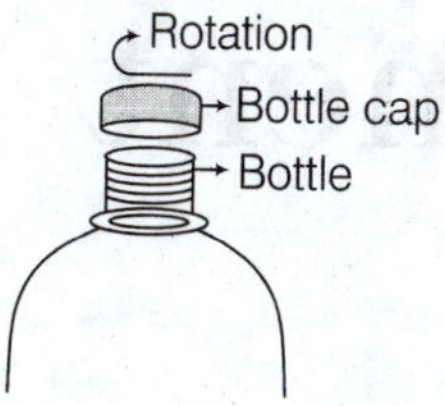

(a) A wedge (b) Wheel and axle
(c) Screw (d) Lever

16. Rahul kicked a football. It rolls on the ground and after covering some distance stops. The force which stops the ball is

(a) muscular force
(b) mechanical force
(c) gravitational force
(d) frictional force

17. Who am I?

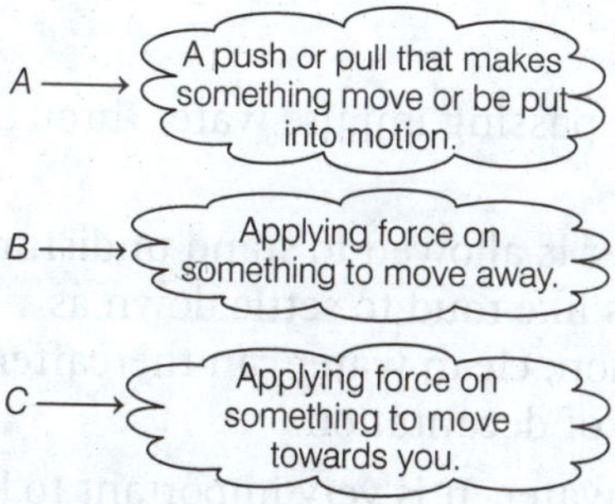

	A	B	C
(a)	Push	Pull	Force
(b)	Force	Push	Pull
(c)	Pull	Force	Push
(d)	Push	Force	Pull

18. *X* enables work to be done. There are many forms of *X*. What is *X*?

(a) Energy
(b) Sun
(c) Heat
(d) Sound

19. What will be the effect of gravity on each of the following activities?

	Activity I	Activity II
(a)	Gravity slows him down.	Gravity slows her down.
(b)	Gravity speeds him up.	Gravity slows her down.
(c)	Gravity slow him down.	Gravity speeds her up.
(d)	Gravity speeds him up.	Gravity speeds her up.

20. Refer to the given Venn diagram and select the correct option regarding it.

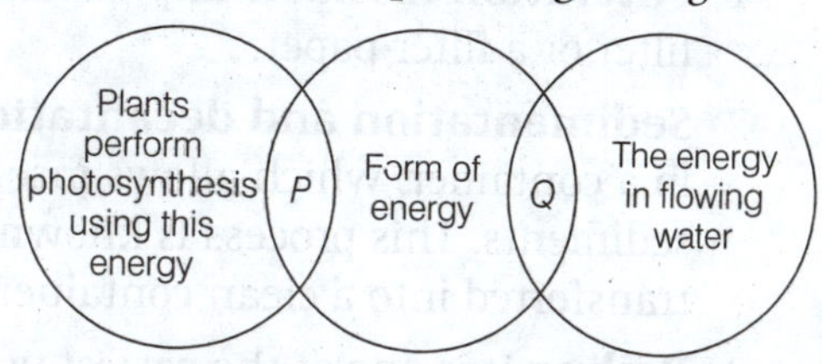

	P	Q
(a)	Wind energy	Hydro energy
(b)	Solar energy	Wind energy
(c)	Solar energy	Water energy
(d)	Geothermal energy	Solar energy

Chapter 08

Our Environment

Our environment mainly consists of air, water and soil.

Air

- Air is a mixture of gases like Nitrogen (71%), Oxygen (21%), Carbon dioxide, water vapour, etc.
- The Earth is surrounded by a blanket of air, which we call the **atmosphere**.

Water

- About three fourth part of our Earth's surface is covered with water in all three states: Water, snow and water vapour. That is why our Earth is called as **Blue planet**.
- The recycling of water in all three states by evaporation, condensation and precipitation in the nature is called **water cycle**.

Method of Purification of Water

1. **Filteration** Insoluble impurities are removed by passing impure water through a filter or a filter paper.
2. **Sedimentation and decantation** Impure water is allowed to stand undisturbed in a container, which allows insoluble impurities like mud to settle down as sediments. This process is known as sedimentation, clean water can thereafter be transferred into a clean container by the process of decantation.
3. **Boiling** It is one of the easiest way of purifying water. It is very important to boil water at 100°C for at least 10-15 minutes to kill harmful microorganisms and germs.
4. **Addition of chemical tablets** Chemicals like chlorine tablets or Potassium permagnate can be added to water tanks to kill harmful germs and bacteria.

Soil

- Top most layer of the Earth's surface is called soil. Soil is made up of different layers, i.e. topsoil (humus), subsoil, parent material layer and bedrock layer.

- Clayey soil has maximum water holding capacity whereas sandy soil has the least water holding capacity. Loamy soil is best for the growth of plant.
- The removal of top most layer of soil by wind or water lead to **soil erosion**. Plant helps to prevent soil erosion.

Greenhouse Effect and Global Warming

- **Greenhouse effect** is the warming of Earth's atmosphere by traping heat from Sun by gases like CO_2 and methane, which are known as greenhouse gases.
- Due to excess increase in these gases, the temperature of Earth is gradually increasing which lead to **global warming**.
- **Ozone layer depletion** is thinning of the ozone layer present in the upper atmosphere.

Pollution

It is mainly of three types

- **Air pollution** Factories release harmful chemicals in air, burning of fossil fuels, burning fire crackers this lead to air pollution.
- **Water pollution** It occurs, when toxic substance enter lakes, rivers, ocean and other water bodies release of hot water and sewage into water bodies.
- **Soil pollution** It occurs, when we dump garbage here and there, use of harmful chemicals in crop fields and uses plastic bags.

Let's Practice

1. This is the symbol of 3R's. What does these R represent?

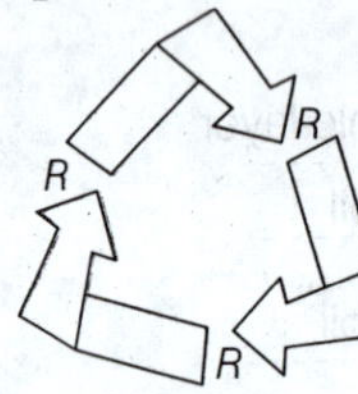

(a) reduce, reuse, recycle
(b) reduce, resume, recycle
(c) reset, reuse, recycle
(d) reset, resume recycle

2. Which type of harmful wastes are released by industry?
(a) Hot water and liquid chemical wastes
(b) Soap water
(c) Rainwater
(d) All of the above

3. What is this phenomenon of increase in Earth's temperature known as
(a) global warming (b) earth's warming
(c) sun's tropping (d) light house effect

4. What result the given activity will have on the environment?

(a) Gives out carbon dioxide in the air, so oxygen reduces
(b) Gives out oxygen in the air, so carbon dioxide reduces
(c) Gives out nitrogen in the air, so oxygen reduced
(d) Gives out energy in the air, so gases are reduced

5. How does Earth's temperature increase due to increase in concentration of pollutant?
(a) They trap sun's heat and does not allow it to escape
(b) They themselves emit heat
(c) They cause forest fires and thus heat up the atmosphere
(d) All of the above

6. What from the following is unexpected weather changes due to rise in pollution?
(a) Snowfall in Saudi Arabia
(b) Widespread floods in Europe
(c) Very heavy snowfall in Kashmir
(d) All of the above

7. Match the following columns.

Column I		Column II
A. Ozone	1.	Harms surfaces of buildings and soil
B. Acid rain	2.	Rise in temperature of Earth
C. Pollution	3.	Protects from harmful ultraviolet rays of the Sun
D. Green house effect	4.	Contamination of the environment with harmful substances

Codes

	A	B	C	D
(a)	1	3	2	4
(b)	1	2	3	4
(c)	3	1	4	2
(d)	4	2	3	1

8. Why does 'Kabari wala' buy old newspapers and magazines from us?
(a) They resell them in the villages and earn money
(b) They sell it to the factories which make fresh paper from the old papers
(c) They burn them to warm up the cold areas
(d) They make envelopes from them

9. Which process in the water cycle shown given below is not correctly labelled?

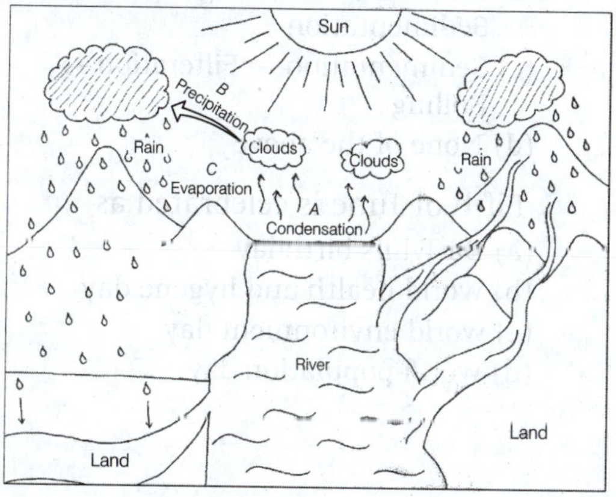

(a) A - Condensation (b) B - Precipitation
(c) C - Evaporation (d) All of these

10. Rhea saw a hospital staff putting a chemical tablet in all watertanks. What could be that tablet of?
(a) Carbon (b) Oxygen
(c) Chlorine (d) Fluorine

11. Match the following columns.

	Column I		Column II
A.	Burning	1.	Garbage dumped in the open away from a town or city
B.	Composting	2.	Garbage dumped in the deep ditches, which are dug in the ground
C.	Landfills	3.	Garbage is collected and burnt
D.	Open dumping	4.	Degradable waste dumped into a pit to convert into manure

Codes

	A	B	C	D
(a)	1	3	2	4
(b)	2	3	4	1
(c)	3	4	2	1
(d)	4	2	3	1

12. Dead leaves are important for soil because
(a) they help the arrival of new leaves
(b) they form manure
(c) they provide colour to soil
(d) None of the above

13. Rohan want to make a pot for his mother which types of soil should he choose?
(a) Sandy soil (b) Loamy soil
(c) Clayey soil (d) Any soil

14. Read the following statements.
I. We can control pollution within few days.
II. Factories should use filters that clean the air before released in atmosphere.
III. CNG should be used in the vehicles
IV. Air pollutants like dust and dust particles may reduce vision.

Choose the correct option.

	I	II	III	IV
(a)	F	T	F	T
(b)	F	F	T	T
(c)	T	F	F	F
(d)	F	T	T	T

15. Classify the following sources of pollution into three classes based on which type of pollution do they cause?

Burning of fuels, soil erosion, landfills, mining, fertilisers, automobiles

	Air pollution	Soil pollution	Water pollution
(a)	Burning of fuels, automobiles	Landfills, mining	Fertilisers, soil erosion
(b)	Burning of fuels, soil erosion	Fertilisers, mining	Landfills, automobiles
(c)	Mining, fertilisers	Landfills, soil erosion	Burning of fuels, automobiles
(d)	Landfills, automobiles	Burning of fuels, soil erosion	Mining, fertilisers

16. Which of the following pollutant may be responsible for such increase in temperature on Earth?

(a) Oxygen (b) Carbon dioxide
(c) Hydrogen (d) Nitrogen

17. Tia took water sample from the nearby lake. Which among the following options is correct order to purify the lake water?

(a) Sedimentation → Boiling → Filteration
(b) Filteration → Boiling → Sedimentation
(c) Sedimentation → Filteration → Boiling
(d) None of the above

18. Fifth of June is celebrated as

(a) Darwin's birthday
(b) world health and hygene day
(c) world environment day
(d) world population day

Chapter 09

Natural Resources

A material found in nature that has usefulness and economic value such as trees, water, minerals is known as **natural resources.**

Types of Natural Resources

They are classified into two groups that is renewable source and non-renewable source.

1. Renewable Source

The amount of these resources can be regained by the efforts of people after they get exhausted. Some examples are

- Solar energy is a renewable source of energy, which we get from sunlight.
- Wind and hydro energy is also a renewable source of energy, which helps in the production of electricity.

2. Non-renewable Source

The amount of these resources are limited. They can be exhausted by human activities and never be regained. Some examples are

- **Fossil fuel** These were formed from the dead remains of living organisms (fossils), like coal, petroleum and natural gas.
- **Coal** are formed when plants get buried under the soil for many years as more soil deposited over them these dead plants slowly got converted into coal. Then, they are taken out by mining.
- **Petroleum and natural gas** are formed from organisms living in the sea. As these organisms died, their bodies settled at the bottom of the sea and get covered with layers of sand and clay. Over the years dead organisms transformed into petroleum and natural gas.
- **Mineral** is a naturally occurring solid with a definite shape but generally do not have fixed composition. These are formed over millions of years in a star.

Let's Practice

1. Which of the following is not a fossil fuel?

Natural gas (a) Coal (b) Solar energy (c) Oil (d)

2. Which of the fossil fuels was earliar used in railway engines to produce steam to run the engine?
(a) Natural gas (b) Coal
(c) Petrol (d) Mineral

3. Which one among the following process require solar energy?
(a) Breathing (b) Washing
(c) Photosynthesis (d) Cooking

4. Which among the following is not a renewable source of energy?
(a) Solar energy (b) Hydroenergy
(c) Wind energy (d) Electrical energy

5. Pick the odd one out.
(a) Petroleum (b) Oil
(c) Natural gas (d) Hydro energy

6. Which of these non-renewable resources is used now-a-days in vehicles to reduce pollution?
(a) Petrol
(b) Diesel
(c) Compressed natural gas
(d) All of the above

7. Those source of energy that can be replenished after short period of time are called …… .
(a) renewable source
(b) non-renewable source
(c) solar energy
(d) wind energy

8. Which of the following energy can be used to generate electricity?
(a) Solar energy
(b) Hydro energy
(c) Wind energy
(d) All of the above

9. Which of these wrongly classified?

	Renewable source of energy	Non-renewable source of energy
(a)	Rivers	Solar energy
(b)	Wind	Coal
(c)	Water	Petrol
(d)	Tides	Diesel

10. Read the following statements and choose the correct statement .

Statement I Petroleum and natural gas are formed from organisms living in the sea.

Statement II Minerals are not in solid form.

(a) Statement I is true
(b) Statement II is true
(c) Statement I and statement II are true
(d) Statement I and statement II are false

11. I am a natural resource and you can use me again and again and I can regaind by your effort.

Who am I ?
(a) Renewable source
(b) Non-renewable source
(c) Both (a) and (b)
(d) Either (a) nor (b)

12. Match the following columns.

	Column I		Column II
A.	Petrol	1.	Gaseous fossil fuel
B.	Coal	2.	Liquid fossil fuel
C.	Natural gas	3.	Solid fossil fuel

Codes

	A	B	C		A	B	C
(a)	2	3	1	(b)	1	2	3
(c)	3	2	1	(d)	2	1	3

13. Coal is the form of fossil fuels
(a) Solid (b) Liquid (c) Gas (d) Oil

14. We get hydro energy from
(a) water (b) wind (c) soil (d) sunlight

15. Refer to the diagram and find out the X.

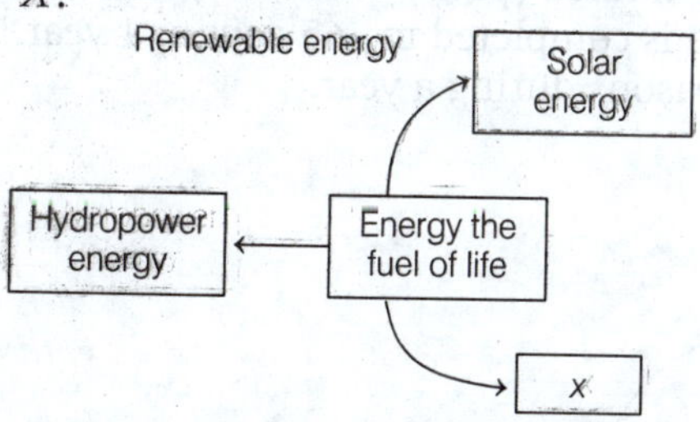

(a) Wind energy (b) Fossil fuel oil
(c) Coal (d) Natural gas

16. Which natural resource should be always available to keep the wind mill moving?

(a) Water (b) Solar energy
(c) Air (d) Plants

17. We should conserve our natural resources. Conservation means wise and careful use of natural resources.

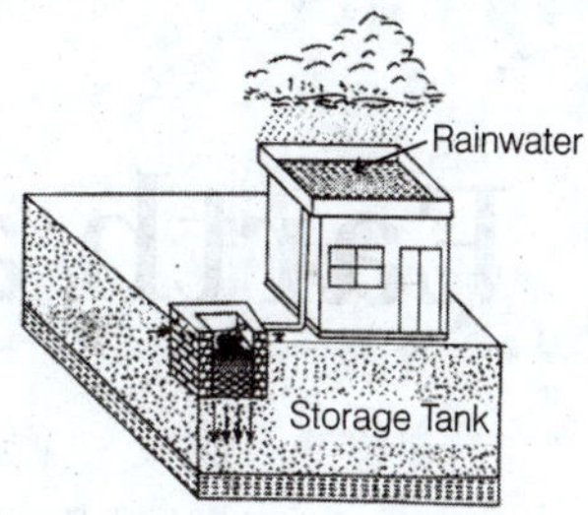

The above picture shows the conservation of which natural resource?
(a) Air (b) Soil
(c) Water (d) Both (b) and (c)

18. Refer to the given Venn diagram and identify X and Y correctly.

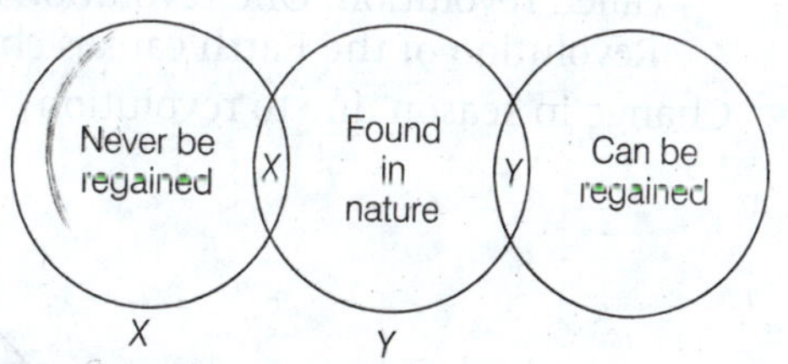

	X	Y
(a)	Sunlight	Coal
(b)	Coal	Air
(c)	Plants	CNG
(d)	Animals	Petrol

19. I am a fossil fuel that is very important for daily use.
I am non-renewable source and regarded as the cleanest source of energy.
I am found deep inside the Earth in the gaseous state.

Who am I?
(a) Petroleum (b) Gasoline
(c) Geothermal (d) Natural gas

Chapter 10

Earth and Universe

Earth

Initially, the Earth was a ball of fire, dust and hot gases, without oceans, land and atmosphere. Gradually, the Earth cooled down, the outer surface of the Earth became hard and the inner core remained hot and molten.

- **Earth has three layers** Crust (outer), Mantle (middle) and Core (inner).
- Earth shows two kinds of movements
  1. **Rotation** Spining of Earth on its axis is called rotation. It takes the Earth 24 hours or a day to complete one rotation. Rotation causes day and night.
  2. **Revolution** The Earth also goes around the sun in fixed (path). This movement is called revolution. One revolution around the Sun is completed in 365 days or 1 year. Revolution of the Earth causes changes in the seasons during a year.
- Change in season due to revolution of Earth

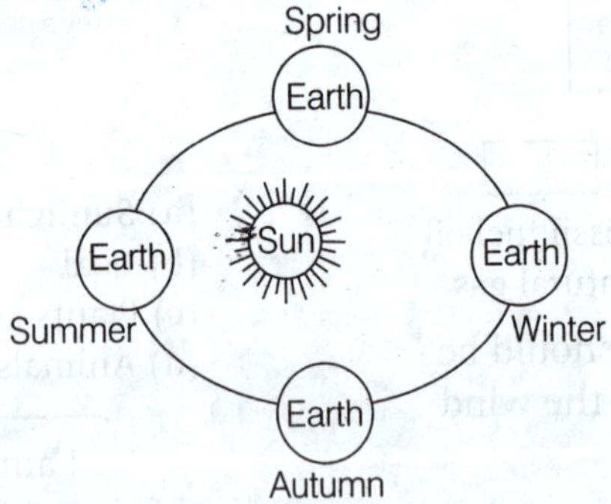

Our Universe/Solar System

- Our universe consists of number of galaxies, stars, planets including our earth and moons.
- The Sun, its planets and all objects moving around them are collectively called as solar system. Our solar system is in a galaxy known as **"the milky way."**
- Our solar system comprises of eight planets. i.e. **Inner planets**: Mercury, Venus, Mars and Earth. **Outer planets**: Jupiter, Saturn, Uranus and Neptune.
- Between inner and outer planets, there is a ring of small bodies, which are made up of rock and metal, these are called **Asteroids**. This ring is also called Asteroids belt.
- A **satellite** orbits or moves around a planet bigger than itself, i.e. Moon is the natural satellite of Earth.
- Sometimes heavenly bodies called **Comets** appear in the sky. They look like stars with a tail.

Let's Practice

1. Arrange the objects given below in increasing order of their size.

   I. Star　　II. Galaxy
   III. Solar system　　IV. Planet

   Choose the correct option.
   (a) II, III, I, IV　(b) III, IV, II, I
   (c) I, IV, III, II　(d) IV, I, III, II

2. Why is it not possible to see Moon and stars during daytime?
   (a) The Moon and stars hide behind the clouds during daytime
   (b) The bright sunlight does not allow to see Moon and stars
   (c) The Moon and stars does not emit light during daytime
   (d) All of the above

3. In which direction Earth revolves around its axis?
   (a) East to West　(b) West to East
   (c) North to South　(d) South to North

4. Consider the following statements about Earth.

   I. Earth takes 24 hours to orbit around the Sun once.
   II. Earth takes 365 days to orbit around the Sun once.

   Choose the correct option.
   (a) Only I　(b) Only II
   (c) Both I and II　(d) Either I or II

5. Which of the following options is the most appropriate reason for changing day and night?
   (a) Revolution of Earth around Sun
   (b) Rotation of Earth around Moon
   (c) Revolution of Earth around Moon
   (d) Rotation of Earth on its own axis

6. Which of the following arrangements shown in the options below correctly depicts the position of Earth-Moon-Sun during a solar eclipse?

(a)

(b)
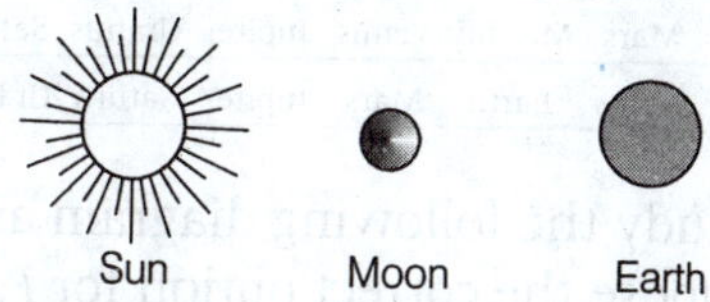

(c)
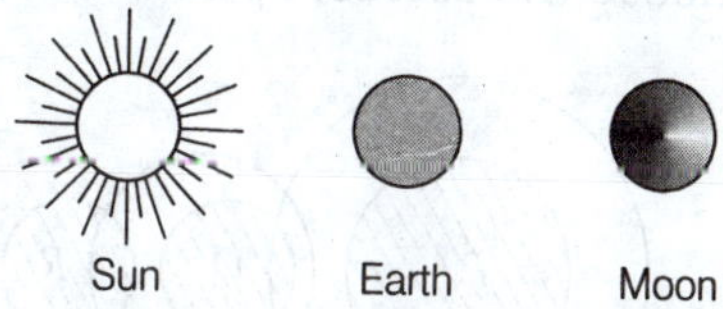

(d)

7. Observe the table given below in which Column I represents some planets and Column II represents their special character. Choose the one which is incorrectly matched.

	Column I	Column II
(a)	Jupiter	Biggest planet
(b)	Saturn	Beautiful rings
(c)	Earth	Rotates sideways
(d)	Neptune	Coldest planet

8. Consider the following statements about a constellation and choose the correct statement.
   (a) It is a group of stars that are close to Earth.
   (b) It is a group of stars that is named after zodiac signs.

(c) It is a group of stars which resembles an unusual animal.
(d) It is a group of stars named for some of recognisable figures seen by astronomers of ancient times.

9. Which of the following options represent the correct sequence of the planets?

	1	2	3	4	5	6	7	8
(a)	Mars	Mercury	Venus	Earth	Uranus	Saturn	Jupiter	Pluto
(b)	Mercury	Earth	Mars	Venus	Saturn	Jupiter	Uranus	Neptune
(c)	Earth	Mars	Mercury	Venus	Jupiter	Uranus	Saturn	Pluto
(d)	Mercury	Venus	Earth	Mars	Jupiter	Saturn	Uranus	Neptune

10. Study the following diagram and choose the correct option for *P*, *Q* and *R*.

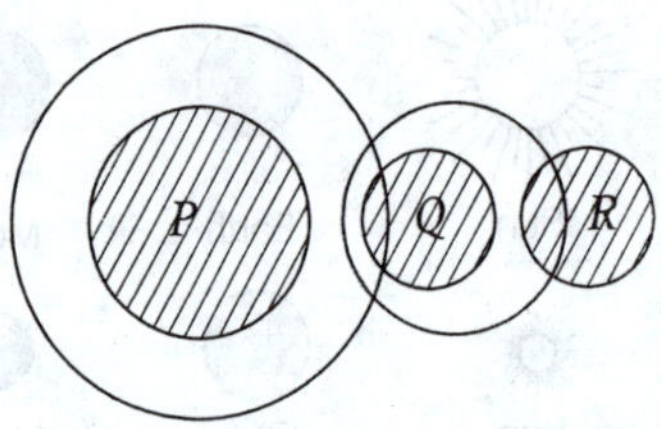

	P	*Q*	*R*
(a)	Sun	Moon	Earth
(b)	Mercury	Venus	Earth
(c)	Sun	Earth	Moon
(d)	Moon	Earth	Sun

11. Match the given matrix in context with the nick names of some of the celestial bodies.

A.	Shooting star	(i)	Comets
B.	Morning star	(ii)	Moon
C.	Blue planet	(iii)	Asteroids
D.	Red planet	(iv)	Meteors
E.	Natural satellite	(v)	Mars
		(vi)	Venus
		(vii)	Earth
		(viii)	Sun

Codes

	A	B	C	D	E
(a)	(vi)	(viii)	(i)	(ii)	(iii)
(b)	(i)	(ii)	(iii)	(iv)	(v)
(c)	(iv)	(vi)	(vii)	(v)	(ii)
(d)	(viii)	(vii)	(vi)	(v)	(iv)

12. Consider the following statements and choose the one which is incorrect in context with the information of our solar system?
(a) Sun is a star around which all the planets orbit.
(b) Our solar system contains nine planets along with their Moons.
(c) Stars and other objects constitutes a solar system.
(d) Both (b) and (c)

13. In which galaxy, does our solar system exists?
(a) Spiral galaxy
(b) Milky way galaxy
(c) Both (a) and (b)
(d) Either (a) or (b)

14. In a solar system, Moons orbit around the
(a) Sun (b) planets
(c) asteroids (d) comets

15. What is axis of the Earth?
(a) It is line passing through Earth
(b) It is the axis present all around the Earth
(c) It is an imaginary line that passes straight from North pole to the South pole
(d) None of the above

16.

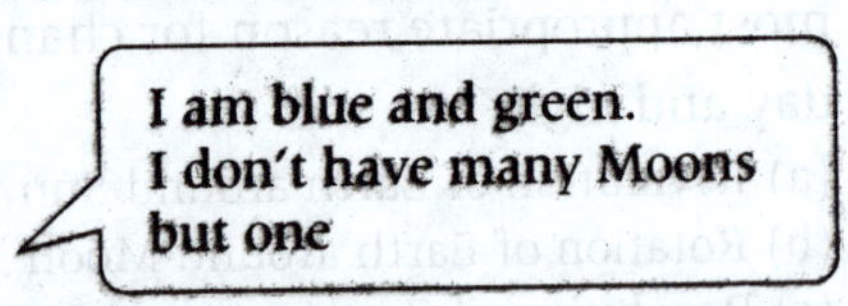

Who am I?

(a) Mars (b) Earth
(c) Venus (d) Neptune

17. Arrange the following in ascending order of their sizes?
(a) Sun < Moon < Earth < Jupiter
(b) Moon < Jupiter < Earth< Sun
(c) Moon > Earth < Jupiter < Sun
(d) Sun < Jupiter < Earth < Moon

18. Read the given conversation among friends and select the correct option.

> *X* is the inner planet of solar system and is also called evening star.

> *Y* is an outer planet of solar system and has maximum number or Moons among all planets.

	X	*Y*
(a)	Mars	Mercury
(b)	Venus	Jupiter
(c)	Moon	Uranus
(d)	Saturn	Earth

19. At which of the four positions *W*, *X*, *Y* and *Z* shown in the figure, would the Moon be during a lunar eclipse?

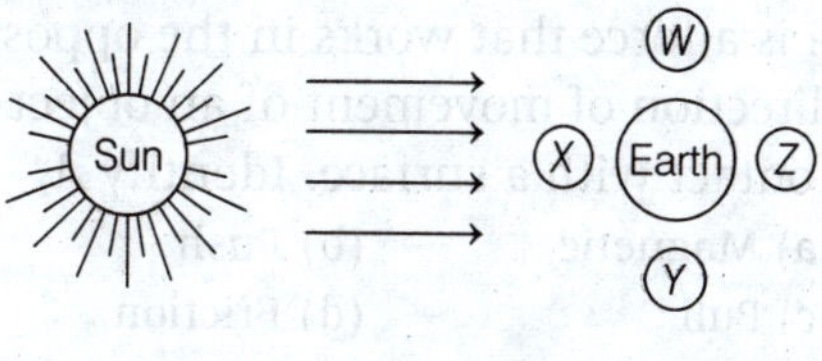

(a) *Z* (b) *W*
(c) *Y* (d) *X*

20. Refer to the given diagram and select the correct option.

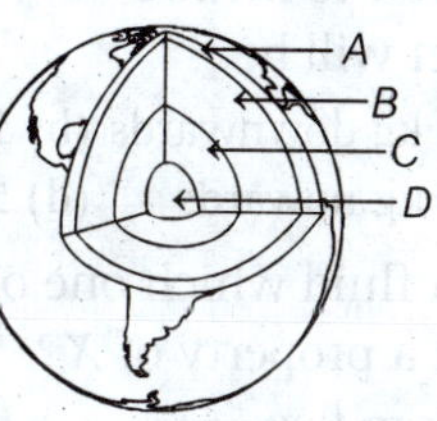

(a) *A* is the outer layer of the Earth
(b) *B* is the innermost part
(c) *C* is below the crust
(d) *D* is made up of nickel–iron mixture

PRACTICE SET 01

1. *A* is a force that works in the opposite direction of movement of an object in contact with a surface. Identify *A*.

(a) Magnetic (b) Push
(c) Pull (d) Friction

2. Rohit used a pulley shown below to lift a bucket of mass 10 kg. The minimum effort required to lift the bucket will be

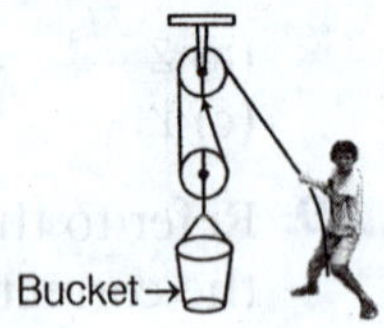

(a) 10 kg downwards (b) 5 kg downwards
(c) 10 kg upwards (d) 5 kg upwards

3. *X* is a fluid which one of the following is not a property of *X*?

(a) It can flow (b) It has mass
(c) It has definite shape (d) We can see it

4. Refer to the given diagram. Identify which statement is correct about *X* and *Y*?

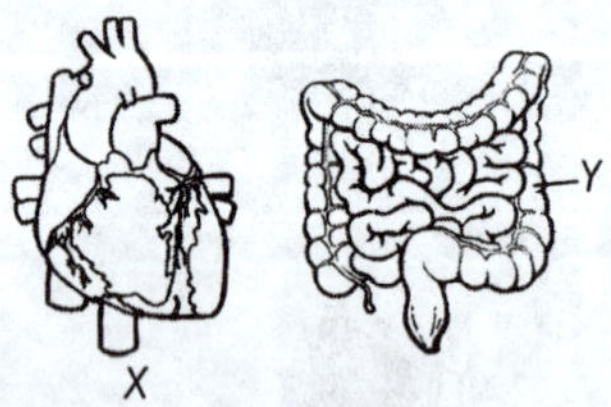

(a) *X* - Part of circulatory system, *Y* - Part of excretory system
(b) *X* - Exchange of gases, *Y* - Digest food components
(c) *X* - Pumping of blood, *Y* - Storage of undigested of food
(d) *X* - Beat continuously, *Y* - Absorption of digested food

5. A camel lives in the desert, a hot and dry place that gets very little rainfall. Which of the following is not their adaptation to survive in such conditions?

(a) They can store food in form of fat in its hump
(b) They have thick lips, so it can eat prickly desert plants without feeling pain
(c) They have black skin colour
(d) They have long eyelashes and extra transparent eyelid to get rid of sand of the desert

6. Circle the odd one out.

(a) Iron nail (b) Gold
(c) Silver (d) Platinum

7. Tiny spores like structure present on the surface of leaf which help in gas exchange are called ......

(a) veins (b) stomata
(c) buds (d) All of these

8. Which layer of soil is suitable for growth of plants?

(a) Topsoil (b) Parent material
(c) Bedrock (d) None of these

9. Given below is the table containing the characteristics of various animals. Choose the animals for which the correct characteristics are mentioned.

Animals	Hair on body	Scales/ feathers	External ears	Internal ears
Fish	Yes	Scales	Yes	Yes
Tiger	Yes	None	Yes	No
Sparrow	Yes	Feathers	No	Yes
Snake	Yes	Scales	Yes	Yes

Choose the correct option.
(a) Tiger and sparrow
(b) Tiger and snake
(c) Dolphin and snake
(d) Dolphin and sparrow

10. Hollow leaves of this plant are filled with nectar. When insects come to drink this nectar, lid closed and they are eaten by the plant. This plant is
(a) lotus (b) pitcher plant
(c) lily (d) water hyacinth

11. Milk and other dairy products come into plastic packaging. Which of the following is the appropriate action to do?
(a) Reuse (b) Recycle
(c) Reduce (d) All of these

12. Consider the set up shown below in which four blocks *A*, *B*, *C* and *D* has been placed in a tank filled with water.

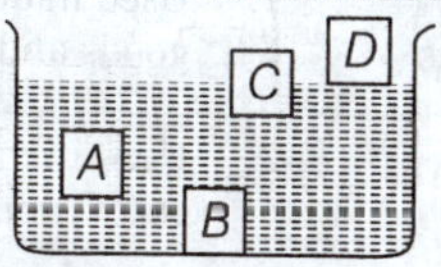

Based on the above experiment following classification has been made.

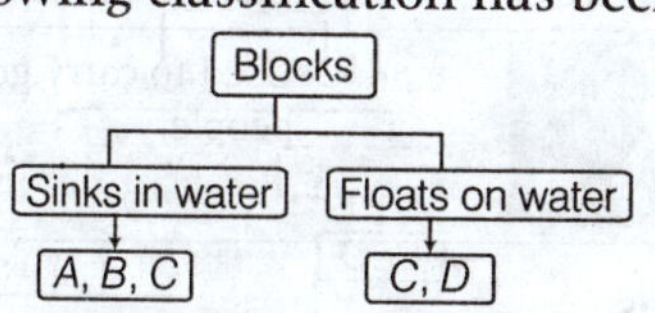

Which of the block is not correctly classified?
(a) *A* should be in floating group
(b) *C* should be in sinking group
(c) *A* and *C* should be in both the groups
(d) Either (b) or (c)

13. I have a tail and gills like a fish, I swim in water but I can jump and hop on land, when I'll grow up. Who am I?
(a) Maggot (b) Nymph
(c) Caterpillar (d) Tadpole

14. I have a crown, I am not a king, I have a neck, I am not an animal.
I have a root, I am not a plant.
Who am I ?
(a) Nail (b) Tongue (c) Tooth (d) Bacteria

15. Which one of the following figure shows the correct rotation of Earth?

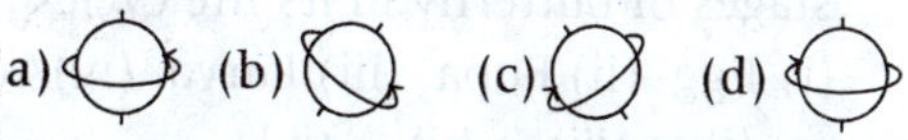

16. The change in season occur due to
(a) Rotation of Earth around its axis
(b) Revolution of Earth around Sun
(c) Revolution of Moon around Earth
(d) Revolution of all planets around Sun

17. Complete the given flow chart and choose the correct option for *X*, *Y* and *Z*.

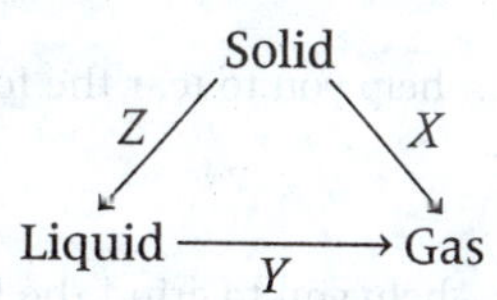

	X	*Y*	*Z*
(a)	Sublimation	Evaporation	Melting
(b)	Melting	Condensation	Evaporation
(c)	Boiling	Melting	Freezing
(d)	Freezing	Melting	Boiling

Direction (Q.Nos. 18-19) We have two sets of teeth during our lifetime. One is milk teeth and the other is permanent teeth.

18. What is the number of milk teeth and permanent teeth in humans?
(a) Milk:20 Permanent:32
(b) Milk:32 Permanent:20
(c) Milk:16 Permanent:10
(d) Milk:15 Permanent:25

19. Out of these two, one is replaced by the other. Choose the correct option.

(a) Milk teeth falls and are replaced by permanent teeth

(b) It depends on person to person

(c) Permanent teeth falls and are replaced by milk teeth

(d) Both falls and are replaced by deciduous teeth

20. Arrange the following according to stages of butterfly in its life cycle

(i) Egg (ii) Pupa (iii) Larva (iv) Adult

(a) (i) → (iii) → (ii) → (iv)

(b) (ii) → (i) → (iii) → (iv)

(c) (i) → (ii) → (iii) → (iv)

(d) (iv) → (ii) → (iii) → (i)

21.  : ...*A*... help you to bite the food.

 : ...*B*... help you to tear the food.

 : ...*C*... help you to grind the food.

 : ...*D*... help you to crack the food.

Codes

	A	*B*	*C*	*D*
(a)	Premolar	Molar	Incisor	Canine
(b)	Canine	Premolar	Molar	Incisor
(c)	Incisor	Canine	Premolar	Molar
(d)	Molar	Incisor	Canine	Premolar

22. Which part of the following do we consume?

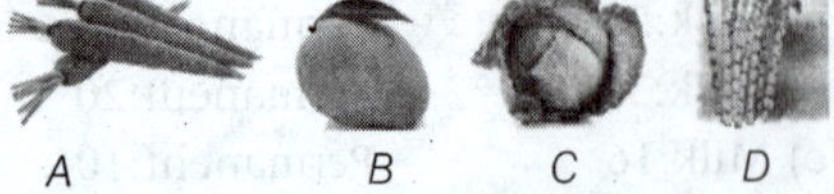

Codes

	A	*B*	*C*	*D*
(a)	Leaf	Root	Stem	Fruit
(b)	Fruit	Leaf	Stem	Root
(c)	Root	Fruit	Leaf	Stem
(d)	Fruit	Stem	Root	Leaf

23. Read the following passage and answer following questions that follow

" Moon has less gravitational force than Earth. The gravity of Moon is 1/6 of the Earth and so, we weigh 6 times less on the Moon than on Earth".

If a person weighs 72 kg on Earth, what will be his weight on Moon?

(a) 12 kg (b) 18 kg

(c) 36 kg (d) 9 kg

24. Match the following pictures of means of transport with their utility.

	Column I		Column II
A.		1.	Used in deserts to carry goods and people.
B.		2.	Used in mountains to carry goods and people.
C.		3.	Used by kings to pull their chariots.
D.		4.	Used to carry goods and people.

Codes

	A	B	C	D		A	B	C	D
(a)	1	3	2	4	(b)	4	3	2	1
(c)	3	1	4	2	(d)	4	2	3	1

25. I have more than, so Moons around me. I am the most beautiful planet having rings in the solar-system.

Who am I?

(a) Jupiter (b) Mars (c) Saturn (d) Earth

26. Study the figure showing two process of purification of water. Choose the correct option for *X* and *Y*.

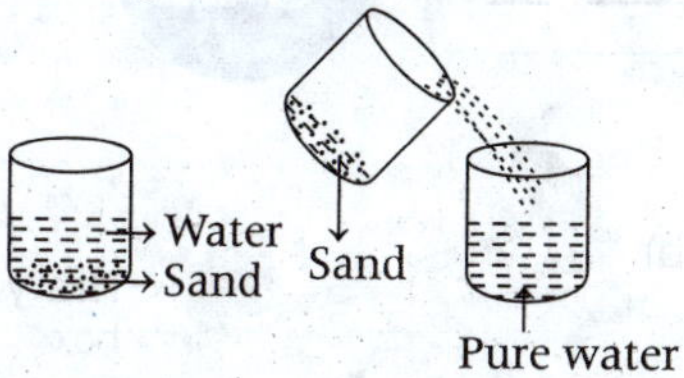

	X	*Y*
(a)	Evaporation	Condensation
(b)	Sedimentation	Decantation
(c)	Decantation	Sedimentation
(d)	Boiling	Chlorination

27. Puja needs an object that does not melt easily and she can see through it clearly. The object should be
(a) Plastic (b) Metal (c) Glass (d) Wood

28. A fan hanging from ceiling falls down and hits the floor with a loud noise. Which of the following shown the energy conversions that have taken place?
(a) Kinetic energy → potential energy → sound
(b) Sound → potential energy → kinetic energy
(c) Potential energy → kinetic energy → sound
(d) Potential energy → sound → kinetic energy.

29. Which of the following is not a cause of soil erosion?
(a) Deforestation (b) Overgrazing
(c) Logging and mining (d) Over population

30. Arrange the following planets which are outside the asteroid belt.
(a) Jupiter → Earth → Venus → Neptune
(b) Pluto → Mercury → Moon → Uranus
(c) Mercury → Venus → Earth → Mars
(d) Jupiter → Saturn → Uranus → Neptune

31. In which of the following food is not stored in the roots of plants?
(a) Carrot (b) Turnip
(c) Sweet potato (d) None of these

32. If Sun disappears suddenly, which of the following will die first and last respectively?
(a) Plants, Humans (b) Humans, Lions
(c) Lions, Plants (d) Plants, Humans

33. Read the following statements and choose the correct option.
Statement I : Trees help in raining.
Statement II : Deforestation causes drought.
(a) Statement I is correct.
(b) Statement II is correct.
(c) Both statements are correct.
(d) Both statements are incorrect.

34. Match Column I with Column II and select the correct option.

Column I	**Column II**
A. Dirty clothes	1. Make you feel cool
B. Warm clothes	2. Protect you from rain
C. Cotton clothes	3. Protect you from cold
D. Waterproof clothes	4. Can make you sick

Codes

	A	B	C	D		A	B	C	D
(a)	4	2	1	3	(b)	4	3	1	2
(c)	4	3	2	1	(d)	3	1	2	3

35. Choose the incorrect statement about first-aid of burn
(a) Cool the burn
(b) Remove rings or other fight items from the burned area
(c) Bandage the burn
(d) All of the above

PRACTICE SET 02

1. Select the forces that the women P and Q in the given picture need to overcome to carry their groceries.

(P) (Q)

	P	*Q*
(a)	Gravity	Friction
(b)	Pull	Push
(c)	Friction	Friction
(d)	Friction	Gravity

2. What is the need of sun in water cycle?

(a) To increase the rate of condensation
(b) To increase the rate of precipitation
(c) To increase the rate of evaporation
(d) To decrease the rate of evaporation

3. Choose the correct option which represents the property and state of a material most appropriately.

	Material	Property	State
(a)	Milk	Definite volume	Gas
(b)	Shampoo	Definite shape	Liquid
(c)	Oxygen	Definite size	Gas
(d)	Salt	Definite shape	Solid

4. Consider the following diagrams and choose the one that does not depict a type of lever.

(a)

(b)

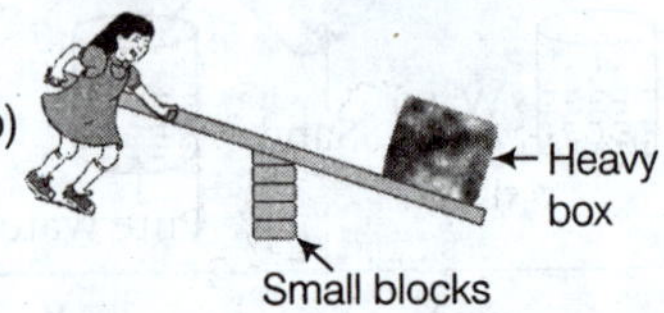

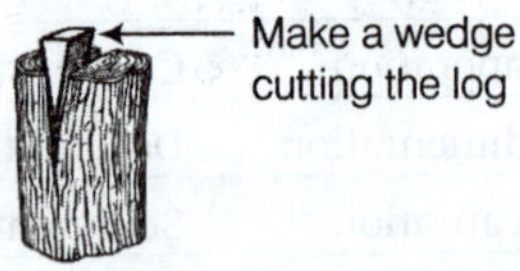

(c)

(d)

5. The process of converting water into water vapour is

(a) diving rod (b) evaporation
(c) blizzard (d) ice crystal

6. Given below is the diagram of respiratory system identify the missing *A*, *B* and *C*.

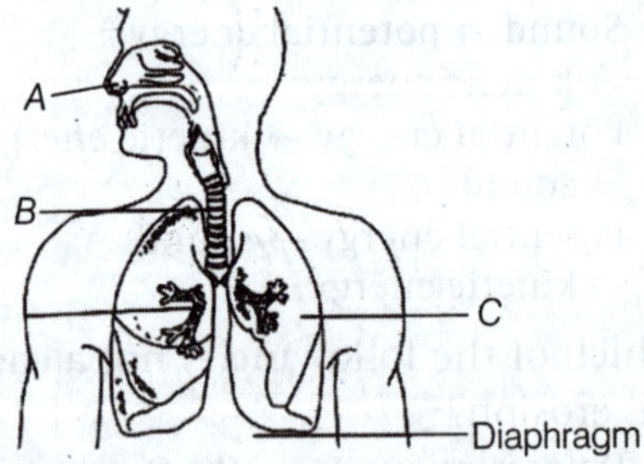

Choose the correct option.

	A	*B*	*C*
(a)	Trachea	Lungs	Nose
(b)	Larynx	Lungs	Nose
(c)	Nose	Trachea	Lungs
(d)	Pharynx	Nose	Lungs

7. Functions of root in plants is/are
(a) absorption of water and minerals from soil
(b) hold the plant frimly in soil
(c) Both (a) and (b)
(d) preparation of food

8. In the particular part(s) of the year, many animals move from one place to another for different reasons. Why do you think these animals especially birds, migrate?
(a) Looking for food
(b) Escaping the extreme seasonal temperatures
(c) Moving to breeding grounds to lay eggs
(d) All of the above

9. Refer to the given flow chart and choose the option which correctly identifies *A*, *B* and *C*.

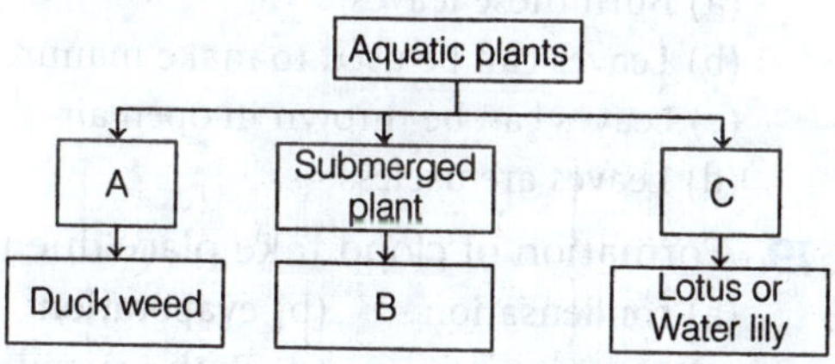

	A	*B*	*C*
(a)	Cedar	Mangrove	Floating
(b)	Fixed	*Hydrilla*	Floating
(c)	Floating	*Hydrilla*	Fixed
(d)	Floating	Water hyacinth	Fixed

10. Somya applies some oil on the hinges of a door. What force is she trying to reduce by adding oil in the hinges?
(a) Friction force (b) Gravity force
(c) Magnetic force (d) Elastic force

11. Which of the following are parasite?
(a) House fly
(b) Honeybee
(c) Lice
(d) All of the above

12. Refer to the given flow chart and select the correct option regarding *X* and *Y*.

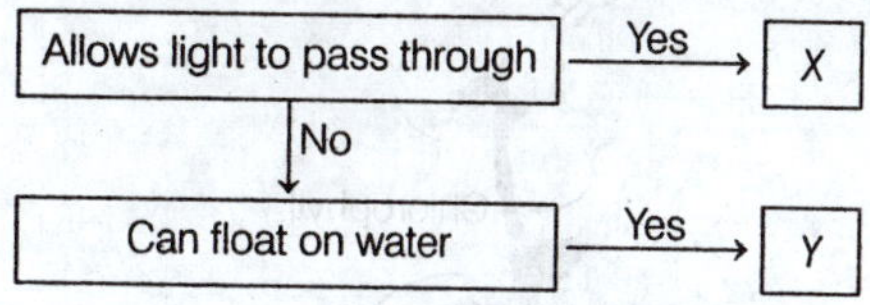

	X	*Y*
(a)	Magnetic	Brittle
(b)	Transparent	Floating
(c)	Lustrous	Mallable
(d)	Opaque	Ductile

13. Which of the following is wrongly matched with their group?
(a) Ants–Colony
(b) Cows–Herd
(c) Owl–Parliament
(d) Deer–Pride

14. If we do not take care of our mouth, we can get toothache. Arrange the following steps causing toothache in correct sequence.
I. Acid creates cavity in teeth causing toothache.
II. Bits of food sticks to the tooth.
III. Germs salt (bacteria) grow in the mouth.
IV. Germs breakdown the food particles which produces acid.

Codes
(a) II, III, IV, I
(b) I, IV, III, II
(c) II, IV, III, I
(d) IV, II, III, I

Direction (Q.Nos. 15-16) Carefully study the diagram drawn by Keshav and answer the following questions.

'Keshav studied photosynthesis process in the class and drew the diagram, but he missed out labelling few components'.

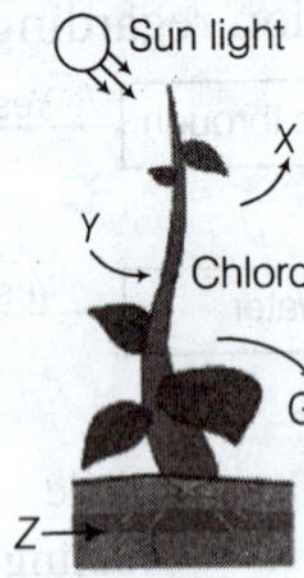

15. What does the arrow Z represent?

(a) Release of water and minerals to the soil
(b) Absorption of water and minerals from the soil by roots
(c) Absorption of carbon dioxide from soil
(d) Release of oxygen into the atmosphere

16. Absorption of carbon dioxide and release of oxygen is represented by which arrow?

(a) X and Y (b) Y and X
(c) Y and Z (d) Z and X

17.

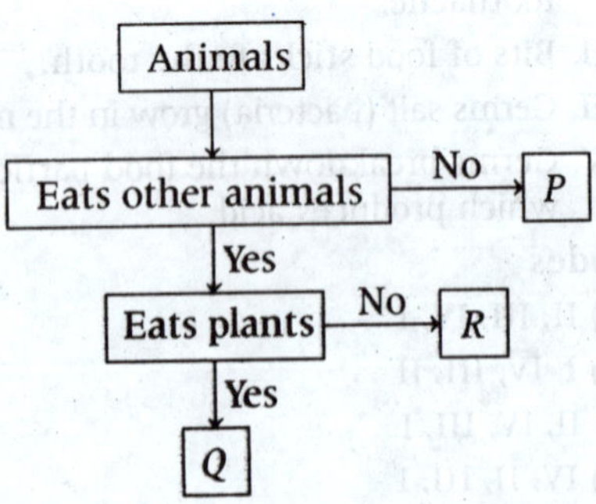

Study the flow chart and choose the option for P, Q and R.

	P	Q	R
(a)	Deer	Lion	Dog
(b)	Cat	Tiger	Deer
(c)	Monkey	Bear	Fox
(d)	Polar Bear	Grasshopper	Snake

18. Look at the picture and predict the best use of this biodegradable dried leaves?

Dried leaves

(a) Burn these leaves
(b) Leaves can be used to make manure
(c) Leaves can be thrown in open air
(d) Leaves are useless

19. Formation of cloud take place due to

(a) condensation (b) evaporation
(c) precipitation (d) Both (a) and (b)

20. An adult frog can breathe through its ...A... in water and with its ...B... on land. It has long hind legs that help it ...C... on land and ...D... feet that help it to swim in water.

Codes

	A	B	C	D
(a)	Gills	Lungs	Crawl	Broad
(b)	Moist skin	Lungs	Move	Flat
(c)	Moist skin	Lungs	Hop	Webbed
(d)	Dry skin	Gills	Sleep	Flipper

21. Match the following columns.

A.  (i) Hand

B.  (ii) Mouth

C.  (iii) Ears

D.  (iv) Eyes

Codes

	A	B	C	D
(a)	(i)	(ii)	(iii)	(iv)
(b)	(ii)	(i)	(iv)	(iii)
(c)	(iii)	(iv)	(ii)	(i)
(d)	(ii)	(i)	(iii)	(iv)

22. Which planet is known as 'Twins of Earth'.
(a) Mars (b) Venus (c) Moon (d) Jupiter

23. Which of the following is paired wrongly?
(a) Dam – Water storage
(b) Rainfed ocean – Brahmaputra
(c) Tubewell – Underground water
(d) River – Ganga

24. Which of the following is not correctly paired?
(a) Lungs – Carbon dioxide
(b) Kidney – Body waste
(c) Immune system – Diseases
(d) Brain – Digestion

25. Acid rain is cause due to
(a) Water pollution
(b) Air pollution
(c) Soil pollution
(d) Soil erosion

26. Match the following columns.

Column I		Column II	
A.	Water	1.	Physical change
B.	Sugar	2.	Solute
C.	Burning of candle	3.	Solvent
D.	Slicing of bread	4.	Chemical change

Codes

	A	B	C	D
(a)	1	2	3	4
(b)	2	3	4	1
(c)	3	2	4	1
(d)	4	1	2	2

27. Select the odd one out on the basis of its mode of reproduction.
(a) Snake (b) Bat
(c) Frog (d) Crocodile

28. Idli is a famous Indian food. The method used to cook it, is …… .
(a) Grilling
(b) Frying
(c) Steaming
(d) Boiling

29. Why does Mukesh prefer to wear white or light-coloured clothes in summer?
(a) White clothes reflect the heat and keep the body warm.
(b) White clothes absorb the heat and keep the body warm.
(c) White clothes absorb the heat and keep the body cool.
(d) These clothes reflect the heat and keep the body cool.

30. Study the given flow chart based on states of matter. Which of the following is correct regarding this?

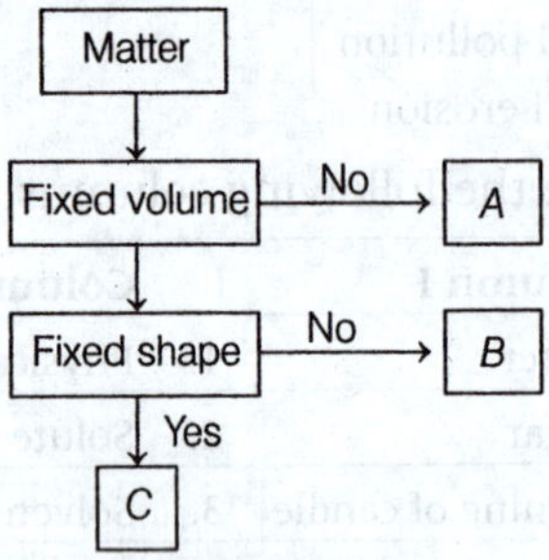

	A	*B*	*C*
(a)	Oxygen	Juice	Wood block
(b)	Oxygen	Wood block	Steel
(c)	Juice	Oxygen	Wood block
(d)	Wood block	Juice	Oxygen

31. Which of the following machines are the same type of simple machines as scissor?

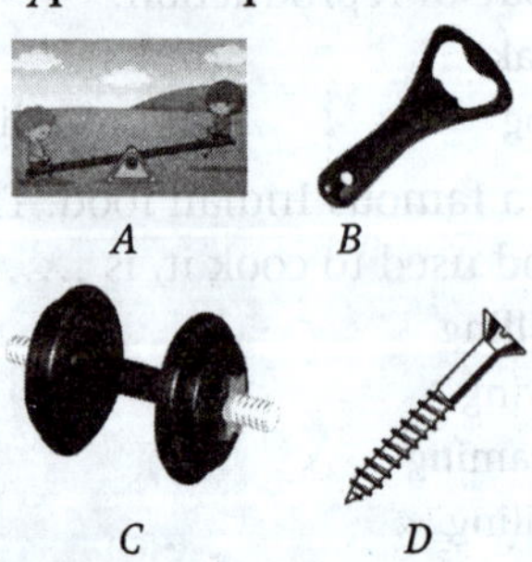

(a) *A* and *B*
(b) *B* and *C*
(c) *C* and *D*
(d) *A* and *D*

32. Which of the following will help to reduce air pollution?
(a) Using electric transport rather than petrol/diesel transport.
(b) Using public transport instead of private vehicles.
(c) Getting vehicles checked for pollution.
(d) All of the above

33. Volcano is an opening on the earth's surface which releases .... when explodes.
(a) crust (b) lava
(c) mantle (d) None of these

34. Match the type of teeth with their no. in mouth of an adult human.

	Types of teeth	No. of teeth
A.	Incisor	1. 8
B.	Canine	2. 4
C.	Premolar	3. 12
D.	Molar	4. 8

	A	B	C	D
(a)	1	2	4	3
(b)	1	4	2	3
(c)	3	1	2	4
(d)	2	1	4	3

35. Laxmi is going to a hilly area for her summer vacation. Which of the following trees will she most probably find there
(a) coconut (b) pipal
(c) spruce (d) None of these

Hints & Solutions

Plants

1. (*b*) *A*-Fibrous root, *B*-Tap root
Fibrous root is a cluster of thin fibre like roots at the base of the stem. These roots spreads out in the soil, e.g. Maize, grass.
Tap root is the main root from which many branching roots grow sideways, e.g. Pea, radish.

2. (*c*) Leaf prepares food for plants, by the process of photosynthesis, in the presence of carbon dioxide, water and Sunlight.

3. (*a*) Plant take carbon dioxide from surrounding and after food preparation they release oxygen.
So, *A*-carbon dioxide and *B*-oxygen.

4. (*d*) A plant can utilise its prepared food in its growth and repairing of damaged parts. Rest of the food is stored in form of starch which animals and humans consumes.
Hence, all options are correct.

5. (*d*) Potato is a stem of plant, it is modified to store food in it.

6. (*c*) Plant store their extra food in the form of starch in leaves.

7. (*a*) Coniferous trees have cones and not flowers. Mangrove trees grow near water bodies, so they have aerial roots to respire. Evergreen trees remain evergreen throughout the year. Deciduous trees shed their leaves in winter season.

8. (*b*) *A*– Shoot system, *B*– Root system
Shoot system lies above the ground. The upper part is exposed to Sunlight. Leaves helps in photosynthesis. Root system lies below the ground. The lower part helps in the absorption of minerals and water.

9. (*c*) The correct equation for the process of photosynthesis is

$$CO_2 + \text{Water} \xrightarrow[\text{chlorophyll}]{\text{Sunlight}} \text{Glucose} + O_2$$

Plant takes CO_2 from the surrounding are water from soil through roots and chlorophyll trap Sunlight then leaf prepares food in form of glucose and O_2 is released as byproduct.

10. (*c*) *Cactus* plants have leaves in the form of thorns, stem of *Cactus* are green and waxy. which allows them to do photosynthesis and prepare their own food.

11. (*c*) Desert plants are not colourless. They do perform photosynthesis but not by their leaves. Their leaves are reduced to prevent loss of water. Their green stems perform photosynthesis.

12. (*c*) Leaves are thin and flat structures found on branches of plants and shed by deciduous trees, in winter.

13. (*b*) Plants need sunlight for their survival and for the preparation of food. Beyond 20 m depth, the sunlight cannot be reached. Hence, it is not possible to survive in a environment where there is no sunlight.

14. (*b*) Plants in hilly areas are coniferous and have needle-like leaves to prevent themself from the damage caused by snow.

15. (*a*) Here, *A* is an orchid which take food and water from the stem of the tree to grow.

16. (*b*) Statements II and IV are incorrect because underwater plants do not have stomata on their leaves, they breathe the dissolved oxygen through their body surface.
The roots floating plants are not fixed at the bottom, the roots just float below the water surface.

17. (*b*) Chlorophyll is the green coloured pigment present in the leaves of the plants and helps in photosynthesis.

18. (*a*) Plants that grow in plains have lots of branches and leaves, they can bear summer heat and shed their leaves in autumn.

19. (*a*) Underwater or submerged plants have no stomata. They use dissolved gases in water through their body surface.

20. (*a*) Water lettuce is a floating aquatic plant and water lily is a fixed plant.

Animals

1. (*a*) Group of elephants is called herd. Group of lions is called pride. Group of monkeys is called band and group of fishes is called school.

2. (*c*) Birds sit on their eggs to keep them warm this process is called as incubation. After some time new young ones hatch out, this is called hatching.

3. (*c*) Bat is a flying mammal, they give birth to young ones and also feed them.

4. (*b*) Dog eats both plant products and animal meat, so its an omnivore. Leech sucks blood from the host animal, so it is called parasite. Elephant eats grass, so it is called herbivore. Lion eats other animals and thus called as carnivore.

5. (*c*) Amphibians can live on land as well as in water. On land they breathe with lungs and in water they breathe through their moist skin.

6. (*b*) The process of shedding old skin by animals is called moulting.

7. (*b*) Bears have black skin colour. As black colour can absorb maximum light, so black skin colour absorb more light to keep their body warm, while polar bears have white fur to escape form its predators.

8. (*b*) *A* – Egg shell, *B* – Yolk, *C* – Albumin
Egg shell is the outer covering of the egg. It protects the egg from harsh conditions.
Yolk is the premature condition of the baby hen (chick). It is rich in fat.
Albumin is the colourless fluid present around the yolk. It is rich in protein.

9. (*c*) Parent bird lays eggs. Parent bird sits on the egg to keep it warm. Embryo develops into chick and chick breaks the shell and comes out when grown.

10. (*a*) Lizard, turtle, snake do not take care of their eggs to provide warmth to the eggs as they are reptiles. Whereas, hen, sparrow and ducks are birds. They sits on their eggs to provide warmth to them.

11. (*d*) A bird have beak but no teeth, it does not help in flying. Flying is done by the use of wings, feathers and body weight. Beak is not a characteristic need for flying.

12. (*b*) The young ones or premature cockroach is known as nymph, The butterfly develops from as cocoon, Tadpole develops into frog and baby bird is known as chick.

13. (*b*) Chameleon exhibits camonflage by changing its colours to suit with its surroundings.

14. (*b*) Monkey, squirrels and Garden lizards are tree dwelling or arboreal animals.

15. (*d*) Butterfly lay eggs on leaves of plants. Eggs then grow into larva, a caterpillar-like stage. This then enters into pupa stage, which grows into adult butterfly.

16. (*d*) A - Moulting, the process of shedding of skin to become adult.
B - Hatching, breaking of egg shell by chick to come out.
C - Reproduction, process, of producing ones own kind.

17. (*c*) The frog is an amphibian. It can live on land and in water.
On land it hop and in water it swim.

18. (*b*) *X* - Birds and *Y* - Insects
Birds have 3 stages in life cycle
Egg → Young ones → Adult
Whereas insect have 4 stages in life cycle
Egg → Embryo → Larva → Adult.

19. (*b*) Polar bears live in North pole, to survive in their environment they have thick furry coat, white in colour which keep them warm.

20. (*b*) In the given food web, the hen is the secondary consumer who can eats both plants and worms and can be eaten by snakes.

Human Body and Its Functioning

1. (*c*) Stomach, food pipe, small intestine are parts of human digestive system, but windpipe is a part of respiratory system.

2. (*b*) Heart belongs to circulatory system which pumps blood.

3. (*c*) The dental formula for human beings is
$$\frac{2123}{2123} \times 2 = 32 \text{ teeth}$$

4. (*a*) 12 pairs of ribs are present in human skeleton system, which protect our delicate organs, i.e. heart and lungs.

5. (*c*) Epiglottis is a thin flap-like structure which prevent the entry of food into windpipe.
Larynx produces sound, oesophagus is tube that conveys food and trachea is windpipe.

6. (*b*) Digestion of protein takes place in stomach. It secretes digestive juices, which break protein into simpler substances.

7. (*c*) Complete digestion takes place in small intestine.

8. (*a*) Kidney filter blood of our body, it remove toxic substances from blood.

9. (*c*) Air which we inhale through our nose has many dust particles along with oxygen which may cause blockage of respiratory system. Small hair in the nose prevents dust particles getting into the respiratory tract.

10. (*c*) Correct sequence of air movement is
Nose → Pharynx → Lungs.

Air enters through our nose then enters into pharynx and then enters into lungs.

11. (*b*) Digestive system is made up of many organs that work together for proper digestion of food. In large intestine, no digestion of food take place. It absorbs water and mineral from undigested food.

12. (*c*) The length of small intestine in human body is 22 feet.

13. (*d*) Statement II is correct, while statement I and III are incorrect because blood carries oxygen (not hydrogen) from heart to all parts of body. Small intestine absorbs all the digestive nutrients and absorption of water occur in large intestine.

14. (*c*) *A* - Lungs
Lungs are those body parts into which oxygen enters and carbon dioxide releases.

15. (*b*) Brain is the part of nervous system and blood vessels are the part of circulatory system.

16. (*c*) Blood vessels carry blood from heart to all body parts and also carry blood from all body parts to heart.

17. (*c*) Bone, it is white, it can broken and there are different types of bones in our body some small and some large.

18. (*a*) Option (a) is correct.
P - Kidney
Q - Ureter
R - Urinary bladder
S - Urethra

19. (*d*) *X* - Premolar, it is used for chewing the food.
Y - Incisor, it is used for cutting and bitting the food.

20. (*a*) Human beings have 2 kidneys.

21. (*b*) Enamel is the hardest part of our body. It is harder than bones.

22. (*d*) Molar, canines and incisors are type of teeth whereas cavity is not a type of teeth. It is a common.

23. (*c*) Saliva gets mixed with the food and makes it easy to swallow. It does not absorbs nutrients.

24. (*a*) Gums present in our mouth holds our teeth.

25. (*c*) Our brain controls all our activities.

Food and Health

1. (*c*) Fats and carbohydrates are the energy giving food. They fulfill our energy requirement in daily life.

2. (*a*) This person is over weight and this condition is termed as obesity. This condition caused due to overeating. Accumulation of fat is also one of the reason which causes obesity.

3. (*b*) Calcium, iron and iodine belongs to group minerals. Vitamins and minerals are protective food and proteins are body building food.

4. (*c*) Here, butter, oil and ghee are source of fats except vegetable, which are source of vitamins and minerals.

5. (*c*) Food have various nutrients that keeps us healthy.

6. (*b*) The body store energy in the form of fats. Excess accumulation of fats is unhealthy.

7. (*c*) The given food item is an egg which contain protein in white part and fats in yolk (yellow) part.

8. (*c*) Vitamin-D is prepared in our body with the help of sunlight.

9. (*c*) Contamination is caused by the entry of germs into drinking water or edible foods.

10. (*a*) Our two-third (about 67%) of body is made up of water. So, 95% is incorrect. All other statements are correct.

11. (*d*) Milk can be preserved by boiling, meat can be preserved by freezing. Peas can be preserved by dehydration and pickles can be preserved by salting.

12. (*a*) Green leafy vegetables, milk and milk products are protective foods. which help us to fight against disease. Potatoes (carbohydrates) are energy giving food. They give energy to do work.
While pulses (protein) are body building food. They helps the body to grow and repair.

13. (*a*) Level-1 food is rich in carbohydrates.
Level-2 food is rich in vitamins and minerals.
Level-3 food is rich in proteins.
Level-4 food is rich in fats.

14. (*b*) Vitamin-A keeps eyes and skin healthy.
Vitamin-B is good for muscles and nerves.
Vitamin-C makes gums strong and heals wounds faster.
Vitamin-D makes teeth and bones strong.

15. (*b*) We should not eat uncovered food from open stalls, street vendors and hawkers because it holds a lot of harmful bacteria, germs dust and flies which may cause various diseases to our body.

16. (*d*) For proper digestion of food we must take care of few things like; we should have food at fixed hours of time. We should eat balanced food. We should eat slowly and chew food well.

17. (*b*) Roughage is a dietary fibre present in fruits, wheat, etc. It helps in removal of waste material from our body.

18. (*c*) Manu made the incorrect statement because roughage are one of the important nutrients which help in removal of waste from our body. Hence, we should take good amount of roughage along with other nutrients in our food.

19. (*d*) Food items which are kept wrongly are in group C because fish and carrot are rich source of vitamin-A, while meat is a good source of protein and vitamin-B.

20. (*a*) *X* - Protein rich components which help in muscle and bone development.
Y - Carbohydrate rich food components which provide energy to our body.

21. (*c*) The boiling of milk kills germs.

22. (*c*) Glucose is a form of sugar or carbohydrates. It gives energy instantly.

23. (*b*) Fats contains the highest amount of energy, followed by carbohydrates and protein respectively. Roughage contain the least amount of energy and provide bulk to our food.

24. (*c*) Carbohydrates and fats are energy giving food, fats have highest amount of energy.

Safety and First Aid

1. (*a*) As fire engine is use to control and extinguish fire, in same way, Ambulance is use to take patients to hospital from the place of accidents or their home.

2. (*b*) In case of minor burn pour cold water on the burnt area then apply anti-burn ointment on it.

3. (*a*) Cotton, adhesive bandage, scissors, aspirin, antiseptic and tweezers should be put in first aid kit.

4. (*d*) A first aid kit for a child should contains cotton, antiseptic lotion, band-aid, antacid (for upset stomach), ORS powder, a thermometer, sticking plaster etc.

5. (*c*) Here, statement III is incorrect and it can be corrected as
Wait for your turn and do not stand in front of the swing. Keep distance from swings.

6. (*c*) Do not touch electric wires, switches and plugs with wet hands. You might get an electric shock which can be fatal.
While touching hot utensils, running in the houses, throwing objects at anyone will not be fatal. But it can harm the human body.

7. (*b*) If there is no footpath, then you should walk on the right side of the road, so that you can see the traffic coming from the front.

8. (*b*) It is advised not to wear nylon cloth, while working in kitchen or lightening crackers because they may catch fire and can harm you. Instead of wearing nylon one should wear cotton clothes.

9. (*d*) Safety rules for children at home are
Do not leave books or toys on the floor.
Do not play around with sharped edged things like scissors, knives and blades and never opens the door to a stranger.

10. (*b*) Option (b) represents zebra crossing which are safe pedestrian crossing.

11. (*c*) The incorrect statement is in option (c).
We should not ignore traffic signals over midnight instead we should always follow traffic rules.

12. (*c*) He should first clean the wound with antiseptic solution and then apply antiseptic cream on it. For small cut, band-aid can also be used.

13. (*c*) Before crossing the road one should always look at your right, then left and then again at right then by using zebra crossing cross the road.

14. (*c*) In case of burn from electricity, immediately take the patiet to the doctor as it may have caused some internal damages. Do not use water in this case. Do not put band-aid either.

15. (*a*) The symbol in option *A* shows traffic lights, option *B* indicates No ovetaking, two way roads are shown by option *C* and no horn zone by option *D*. Option *E* shows slippery road so drive with caution.

16. (*a*) Her mother should remove the sting as early as possible by pressing the surrounding area. After removing the sting, gently wash the affected area with cold water and put on an ice pack over it.

17. (*c*) Both the statement (A) and (B) are correct. One should not play with matchstick or light firecracker on your own. One should never take medicines by himself.

18. (*d*) If there is a leakage in the gas cylinder in kitchen open all the windows and doors to let it go out. Do not touch any electric switch as it may cause fire. Turn off the cylinder (regulator) immediately to stop further leakage.

19. (*b*) Rohit made the incorrect statement because we should fly kites in parks or in open ground but not on the terrace. As one may fall from it.

20. (*d*) While crossing the road at zebra crossing one should not cross the road when the traffic light is green for vehicles.

Matter and Materials

1. (*c*) Matter is anything, which occupies space. Shadow is formed when an object comes in contact with light. It is an image. Heat from the Sun is a form of energy (light energy). It does not occupy space. Hence, both *A* and *C* are not matter. Clouds have mass because the water in it occupies the space. Rain is a form of water and is liquid in nature. It is a form of matter.

2. (*b*) Water when freezes converts into ice which is solid form of water.

3. (*b*) '*X*' represents sublimation. It is the process of direct conversion of solid into gas. For rest options, condensation is the process of conversion of gas into liquid. Freezing is the process of conversion of liquid into solid. Deposition is the process of direct conversion of gas into solid. It is opposite to sublimation.

4. (*b*) '*A*' represents liquid. It has definite volume but do not have definite shape. '*B*' represents gas. It do not have definite shape and volume. '*C*' represents solid. It has definite shape and volume.

5. (*c*) A liquid changes into a gas on heating and the process is called boiling.

$$\text{Liquid} \xrightarrow{\text{Boiling}} \text{Gas}$$

6. (*b*) The picture given shows melting of candle wax.

7. (*d*) Milk is converted into ice cream by the process of freezing. The process of falling down of rain drops from clouds is known as precipitation. Clouds are form by condensation of water vapours. Ice melts to form water (liquid).

8. (*a*) Snowflakes are the solid form of water. They are solid in nature. They have mass, definite shape and definite volume.

9. (*c*) Condensation is opposite process of evaporation. In the same way deposition is the opposite process of sublimation.

10. (*b*) Since, all the three cylinders are made up of different materials, so their mass are different. They all have equal volume of 100 cm^3. Here, all three have definite shape and cannot compressed.

11. (*c*) In the above relation, stone is a solid and lemon juice is liquid. So, in the given option, watch and milk show correct option because watch is solid and milk is liquid.

12. (*d*) Evaporation is the process of conversion of liquid into gas. The puddle that Salman saw disappeared by the process of evaporation take place due to the heat of Sunlight.

13. (*c*) Both group *A* and group *B* materials are of different states of matter and all possess mass too.

14. (*d*) The set up confirms that gases have mass. When balloon *B* got punchured, the air comes out. As a result, the weight of balloon *B* decreases and a disbalance is observed.

15. (*a*) Solid is a state of matter which have mass, shape and volume. Liquids and gases are also state of matter and have mass. But iquids do not have definite shape and gases do not have definite shape and volume.

16. (*c*) Here, matter *C* can be compressed. The matter which does not have fixed volume are gases. They are highly compressible.

17. (*a*) Oil and milk are liquid in nature. They both do not have fixed shape but have fixed volume.

18. (*c*) Matter change from one state to another with change in temperature by heating or cooling.

19. (*d*) The process shown is condensation, The vapours from the tea rise up and reach the lid. Where they get converted back to water droplets.

20. (*c*) Steam (vapours) cools to get converted into liquid state, i.e. water which further cools and freeze in the form of ice.

Work, Force and Energy

1. (*d*) A pulley is a simple machine which consists of a grooved wheel and a rope. It is used to lift things easily.
Lever is also a simple machine but it does not consists of wheel and a rope. Inclined plane is simply a slope over which a load can be pushed up or down. Wheel and axle is a simple machine. It is made up of two circular objects of different sizes.
2. (*b*) A staircase is a type of inclined plane which can be used by a person going to second floor. There are no machines in eating sandwich running across ground and shopkeeper counting money.
3. (*c*) Gravitational force pulls everything down towards the earth, i.e. it acts downwards. In figure 2, the man is jumping down and in figure 4, the dog is running downstairs. Both these actions/activities are done with the support of gravitational force.
4. (*d*) Inclined plane is a simple machine which uses a slanted surface connected from a lower level to a higher level used to carry load through a height.
Wedge is a type of tool with edges are sharp in front and blunt at the back. They are shaped like two inclined planes attached back to back. It is used to cut hard objects. Screw looks like a nail with grooves cut into it. Lever is used to lift weights, cut things and open lids.
5. (*a*) A fork is wedge which consists of two inclined planes joining back to back. Using a wedge, the inclined planes are pushed into the object to tear them apart.
6. (*d*) Height is not considered as a force. Friction, weight and gravity are a form of force. Force is defined as a push or pull of something. Friction is a force which help in stopping the object, weight exert force and gravity is a force which is due to the earth.
7. (*d*) Crane, elevator and well, All use form of pulley system. A pulley system is made from a wheel and a rope. It is used to left things easily.
8. (*c*) Scissor is not a form of wheel and axle. It is a lever. Scissor is a simple machine which is used to cut things.
Car steering wheel and door knob are examples of wheel and axle. These simple machines are made up of two circular objects of different sizes. The wheel is the larger object. It rotates around the smaller circular object called axle.
9. (*c*) Inclined plane is the simple machine which is used by the Geeta. An inclined plane is a simply a slope over which load can be pushed up or down. Wedge is not used by Geeta because a wedge is a simple machine as like of knife whose edges are sharp in front and blunt at the back. Staircase is a type of inclined plane.
10. (*a*) Statements 1 and 3 are incorrect or false and they can be corrected as,
Friction develops when two things are in contact. We cannot walk without friction.
11. (*c*) Claw hammer is a lever whereas a screw driver and door knob both are wheel and axle type of simple machines.
12. (*a*) The diagram shows a lever. Here, scissor is a lever. Cycle is a wheel and axle type machine. Staircase is an inclined plane and a screw is a simple machine which is a nail with grooves cut into it.
13. (*a*) A claw hammer is a lever which is used to pull apart a nail from the wall. A wedge such as claw ended hammer is used to push a nail in the wall or in an object.
A lever such as screw driver is used to put the screw in the wall or in hard object.
14. (*c*) In figure I, the boy is pushing the wall, therefore applying the force, In figure II, the boy is carrying the heavy box, therefore applying the force. In figure III, Neither pull or push is applied by anyone, therefore, book is lying on the able.
15. (*c*) Screw is the simple machine which is used in a bottle cap. Screw look like a nail with grooves cut into it. It is used to hold things together. Bottle cap are design as screw.
16. (*d*) The force which stops the ball or which opposes the motion is called frictional force.
17. (*b*) A → A push or pull that makes something move or be put into motion is called force.
B → Applying force on something to move away is called push.
C → Applying force on something to move towards you is called pull.

18. (*a*) The capacity to do work is called energy. Energy is available in different forms such as heat energy, light etc.
19. (*c*) The boy who is climbing uphill is working against gravitational force, so gravity will slow him down. On the other hand a girl skiing downhill is working towards the direction of gravitational force, so gravity will speed her up.
20. (*c*) Plants perform photosynthesis using energy from sun called solar energy and the energy in flowing water is known as water energy.

Our Environment

1. (*a*) The three R's widely used for the reduce, reuse and recycle. The motto of this 3R's is to remove waste material from environment.
2. (*a*) Hot water and liquid chemical wastes are released by industry. Soap water is usually released by homes and rainwater is the natural form of water.
3. (*a*) The trapping of Sun's heat in the atmosphere is known as greenhouse effect and due to excess amount of gases like CO_2, the increase in Earth's temperature is known as global warming.
4. (*a*) The man is putting on the fire using wood which is basically a form of carbon. When woods are exposed to fire in the presence of air. The formation of carbon dioxide takes place, which will increase in the concentration of carbon dioxide and results in decrease in the concentration of oxygen in the air and lead to air pollution.
5. (*a*) Pollutant trap Sun's heat and does not allow it to escape. Due to the presence of pollutants such as dust and smoke, the rays which coming from Sun remains on the Earth. This results in the warming of Earth.
6. (*d*) Snowfall in Saudi Arabia, widespread floods in Europe, very heavy snowfall in Kashmir all are the unexpected weather changes due to the rise in pollution.
7. (*c*) Ozone protects from harmful Ultraviolet rays of the Sun.
   Acid rain harms surfaces of buildings and soil.
   Greenhouse effect causes rise in temperature of Earth.
   Pollution is contamination of the environment with harmful substances.
8. (*b*) 'Kabari wala' buys old newspapers and magazines from us to sell it to the factories, which make fresh paper from the old ones by recycling process.
9. (*d*) The correct labelling should be
   A - Evaporation is a process in which water from the lakes, rivers evaporates and turns into water vapour.
   B - Condensation is a process in which water vapours condenses to form clouds.
   C - Precipitation is a process by which the cloud give shower of water droplets.
10. (*c*) Chlorination is a process of purification of water using chlorine tablets.
11. (*c*) Burning is burning of garbage collected at one place. Composting is when degradable waste dumped into a pit to convert into manure.
    Open dumping is a method in which garbage dumped in the open, away from a town or city.
    Landfills is dumping of garbage in the deep ditches, which are dug in the ground.
12. (*b*) Dead leaves are important for soil because they become humus and provide manure and nutrients to soil.
13. (*c*) Clayey soil has the highest water holding capacity which help in making pots giving.
14. (*d*) I statement is false. It is corrected as We cannot control pollution in few days. Once the pollution increases this is very difficult to control the side effects of it.
15. (*a*) Burning of fuels, automobiles — Air pollution
    Landfills, mining — Soil pollution
    Fertilisers, soil erosion — Water pollution.
16. (*b*) Carbon dioxide has the capacity to trap Sun's heat and not letting it escape out from the atmosphere. It is released by automobile and burning of fuels. So, it is the main pollutant that is responsible for such an increase of temperature.
17. (*a*) Lake water is drinking water but it may contain mud, bacteria etc. Lake water is left for sedimentation for few hours and then boiled for 10-15 minutes. It is then filtered out with the help of a filter paper.
18. (*c*) Fifth of June is celebrated as world environment day.

Natural Resources

1. (c) Solar energy is an example of renewable source, whereas all the other three options are source of non-renewable and forms of fossil fuel.
2. (b) Earlier, coal was used in railway engines to produce steam to run the engine. Now-a-days diesel is used as fuel in railway.
3. (c) Photosynthesis, require solar energy to make food for plants.
4. (d) Electrical energy is not a renewable source of energy whereas solar energy, hydro energy and wind energy is a source of renewable source of energy.
5. (d) Hydro energy is the odd one because it is an example of renewable source of energy, whereas other three are non-renewable soruce of energy.
6. (c) Compressed Natural Gas (CNG) is used to run vehicles. It is used as a substitute of petrol and diesel and causes very less pollution.
7. (a) Those source of energy that can be replenished after short period of time are called renewable source.
8. (d) Solar energy, hydro energy and wind energy can be used to generate electricity. Solar energy can be generated as long as sun shines, Hydro energy can be generated by water flow and wind energy can be generated by air.
9. (a) Solar energy is not a non-renewable source of energy. It is a renewable source of energy. Renewable source of energy is defined as the energy, which can be renewed easily.
10. (a) Statement I is correct and II is incorrect. Petroleum and natural gas are formed from organisms living in the sea. Minerals are present in solid form under the soil.
11. (a) Renewable source is a natural resource and you can use it again and again and you can also regain it by your (people) efforts.
12. (a) Petrol is a liquid fossil fuel, which we use in our cars.
    Coal is a solid fossil fuel which we use in cooking and power plant.
    Natural gas is a gaseous fossil fuel, which is used in industrial process.
13. (a) Coal is the solid form of the fossil fuels which is formed, when plants get buried under the soil.
14. (a) Hydro energy is a form of renewable energy that uses the power of moving water to generate electricity.
15. (a) Wind energy is the form of renewable source of energy and all the remaining three options are source of non-renewable energy.
16. (c) Moving air helps the wind mill to rotate and generate electricity. When it rotates the energy of wind converts into rotational energy. The rotation of blades causes the turbine to move, which helps in the generation of electricity.
17. (c) Water conservation is done in this picture, the technique is known as rainwater harvesting. A house roof is used to store the rainwater. It can be used latter for various purpose.
18. (b) Thing which are found in nature are called natural resources and they are classified mainly in two groups, first one is renewable source, which can be regained by efforts. e.g., Air (Y), plants, animals and second one is non-renewable source, which cannot be regained like coal (X), CNG, petrol.
19. (d) Natural gas is a fossil fuel that is very important for daily use and it is non-renewable source and regarded as the cleanest source of energy and found deep inside the Earth in the gaseous state.

Earth and Universe

1. (d) Galaxy contains stars and solar system. Solar system contains Sun, eight planets, their Moons and other celestial bodies.
   So, option (d) is correct in context with the increasing order of their size.
2. (b) Moon is a non-luminous object whereas, stars are luminous but very far away from the Earth. When the bright sunlight strikes Earth, it makes it impossible for light from other stars to be distinguished and hence, we do not see stars and Moon during daytime.
3. (b) The Earth revolves around its axis from West to East direction due to which Sun appears to rise in East and sets in West direction.
4. (b) The correct statement for I is Earth takes 24 hours to rotate on its own axis once. The process is called as rotation.
5. (d) Rotation of Earth upon its axis causes some part of Earth lightened by sunlight thereby causing variation of day and night.

6. (*b*) During a solar eclipse, Moon comes between Sun and Earth and shadow of Moon falls on Earth. Also, we have to consider the size of all the three bodies. Sun is largest among them and Moon is the smallest.
7. (*c*) Uranus is the only planet that rotates sideways all other statements are correct.
8. (*d*) As constellation is a group of stars named for some recognisable figures which was seen by astronomers in ancient times.
9. (*d*) The correct sequence is Mercury, Venus, Earth, Mars, Jupiter, Saturn, Uranus and Neptune.
10. (*c*) The given picture shows *P* as Sun, around which *Q*-Earth revolves and *R* represent Moon which revolves around Earth. Also the size of Sun is largest among them and size of Moon is smallest among them.
11. (*c*)

A.	Shooting star	(iv)	Meteors
B.	Morning star	(vi)	Venus
C.	Blue planet	(vii)	Earth
D.	Red planet	(v)	Mars
E.	Natural satellite	(ii)	Moon

12. (*d*) Our solar system contains eight planets and their Moons. There is only one star in our solar system, i.e Sun.
13. (*b*) Our solar system exists in outer spiral of Milky way galaxy.
14. (*b*) Moons are the natural satellites, which orbit around the planets.
15. (*c*) Axis of the Earth is an imaginary line that passes straight from North pole to the South pole.
16. (*b*) Earth is blue and green in colour because of the presence of water and trees on its surface and Earth have only one Moon.
17. (*c*) Moon is smaller than Earth. It is the natural satellite of Earth hence revolves around it. Jupiter is largest planet of solar system. Sun is the star of the solar system around which all the planets rotates.
18. (*b*) *X* is Venus which is inner planet of solar system and is also called evening star and Y is Jupiter which is outer planet of solar system and has maximum number of Moons among all planets.
19. (*a*) A lunar eclipse occurs when the Earth comes between the Sun and the Moon. The earth casts a shadow on the Moon due to which we cannot see it.
20. (*a*) A is the outer layer of the Earth, which is crust and *B* is mantle which is below the crust, core is a thick layer of rocks rich in iron and magnesium. It is further divided into a liquid outer core (*C*) made up of nickel-iron mixture and inner core (*D*) made up of iron.

Practice Set 1

1. (*d*) Frictional force opposes motion because it acts in the direction opposite to the direction of the movement of an object.
2. (*b*)
3. (*c*) Liquids are also known as fluid due to its ability to flow. It has mass and we can see it. It do not have definite shape but have fixed volume.
4. (*c*) *X* -Heart is a pumping organ, which pumps blood.
   Y - Large intestine where absorption of water and storage of undigested food takes place.
5. (*c*)
6. (*a*) Iron nail is the material, which get attracted by magnets but all the other three materials are not hence, it is the odd one.
7. (*b*) The tiny spores like structure present on the surface of leaves is called stomata. These helps in exchange of gases in plants.
8. (*a*) Topsoil layer is rich in minerals and organic matter. It is most suitable layer for growth of plant.
9. (*a*)
10. (*b*) Hollow leaves of pitcher plant are filled with nectar. When insects come to drink this nectar, lid closed and they are eaten by the plant.
11. (*b*) Plastics are non-biodegradable. We should always recycle plastic products. This way the pollution due to plastic can be minimised.
12. (*c*) Block *C* is partly sinking and partly floating. Same is the case with block *A*.
13. (*d*)
14. (*c*) A Tooth is divided into 3 parts. The crown, head, the neck part and the root part which fixed in gums.
15. (*b*) The figure (b) shows the correct direction of Earth's rotation, i.e. West to East. Also the axis of Earth is not straight. It is sightly tilted.

16. (*b*) Change in season occurs due to revolution of Earth around the Sun.

17. (*a*) 18. (*a*) 19. (*a*)

20. (*a*) The life cycle of butterfly follows : Eggs → Larvae → Pupa → Adult.

21. (*c*) 22. (*c*)

23. (*a*) Gravity of Moon is 1/6 than Earth. So, pull is also 1/6 of Earth. Therefore, a body will weigh 6 times less on Moon as on Earth. Therefore, if a body weighs 72kg on Earth, its weight will be 1/6 of it, i.e. 72/6 = 12kg.

24. (*c*)

25. (*c*) Jupiter and saturn both have more than 50 Moons revolving around them. Saturn has a beautiful structure of rings. Hence, saturn is the most beautiful planet in the solar-system.

26. (*b*)

27. (*c*) Glass is a material that does not melt easily and is transparent. While plastic melt easily, but it can be transparent.

28. (*c*)

29. (*d*) Overpopulation does not cause soil erosion. Overgrazing, deforestation reduces green plants and this causes soil erosion. By logging and mining the soil erosion takes place.

30. (*d*) Asteroid belt lies between Mars and Jupiter, hence the outside planets are. Jupiter → Saturn → Uranus → Neptune.

31. (*d*) Unlike potato, sweet potato stores its food in the roots.

32. (*d*) 33. (*c*) 34. (*b*)

35. (*d*) All the statements are correct about first aid of burn.

Practice Set 2

1. (*d*)

2. (*c*) Sun provides heat energy which increases the rate of evaporation of water.

3. (*d*) 4. (*c*)

5. (*b*) The process of converting water into water vapour is called evaporation.

6. (*c*) *A* - Nose, *B* - Trachea, *C* - Lungs

7. (*c*) Function of root in plants is to hold the plant firmly in soil and absorption of water and minerals from soil.

8. (*d*) 9. (*c*) 10. (*a*)

11. (*c*) Lice is a parasite, they feed on human blood for their nutrition.

12. (*b*) Materials that allow light to pass through them called transparent and materials that can float on water is called floating.

13. (*d*) 14. (*a*)

15. (*b*) Absorption of water and minerals from the soil by roots. Roots are present in the soil. Soil have rich minerals and water. The function of roots is to absorb those minerals and transport it to the upper part of the plant.

16. (*b*)

17. (*a*) *P* : Deer is a herbivore, who eats only plants.
R : Lion is a carnivore, who eat other animals but not plants.
Q : Dog is omnivore who eats both plants and animals.

18. (*b*) 19. (*d*)

20. (*c*) An adult frog can breathe through its moist skin in water and with its lungs on land. It has long hind legs that help it hop on land and webbed feet that help it to swim in water.

21. (*b*) A. (ii) B. (i) C. (iv) D. (iii)

22. (*b*) Venus is known as Earth twin because of similar size same mass.

23. (*b*) 24. (*d*)

25. (*b*) Acid rain is caused due to the presence of sulphur and nitrous oxide in air, which dissolve with rain water to make it acidic.

26. (*c*)

27. (*b*) Snake, frog and crocodile are egg laying animals, while bat is a mammal that gives birth to young ones.

28. (*c*) Idli is prepared by steaming.

29. (*d*) White clothes reflect the heat and keep the body cool.

30. (*a*) 31. (*a*)

32. (*d*) Air pollution can be reduced by using electric transport, public transport getting vehicles checked for pollution.

33. (*b*)

34. (*a*) There are total 8 incisors, 4 canines, 8 premolars and 12 molar present in mouth of an adult human.

35. (*c*) Spruce is a plant that grows in hilly areas.